THE NEGRO IN GREEK AND ROMAN CIVILIZATION

A STUDY OF THE ETHIOPIAN TYPE

BY
GRACE HADLEY BEARDSLEY, Ph. D.
INSTRUCTOR IN HISTORY AND LATIN IN GOUCHER COLLEGE

Lushena Books
Publishing Chicago,
IL

Lushena Books Publishing
Chicago, IL USA

ISBN 978-1-63923-026-6

© *2021 Lushena Books Publishing*

All rights reserved. No new contribution to this publication may be reproduced, stored in a retrieval system, or transmitted, in any form or by any means, electronic, mechanical, photocopying, recording, or otherwise, without the prior permission of the Publisher.

Printed in the United States of America On 100% Acid-Free Paper

THE NEGRO IN GREEK AND ROMAN CIVILIZATION

A STUDY OF THE ETHIOPIAN TYPE

BY

GRACE HADLEY BEARDSLEY, Ph. D.

INSTRUCTOR IN HISTORY AND LATIN IN GOUCHER COLLEGE

BALTIMORE: THE JOHNS HOPKINS PRESS
LONDON: HUMPHREY MILFORD
OXFORD UNIVERSITY PRESS
1929

FIRST PUBLISHED IN 1929

TO
W. B. H. AND J. W. H.

CONTENTS

CHAPTER		PAGE
	Preface	ix
I.	The Ethiopian in Greek Literature	1
II.	The Introduction of the Ethiopian into Greece	10
III.	The Fifth Century—The Ethiopian Type on Plastic Vases	23
IV.	The Fifth Century—The Ethiopian Type In Vase Paintings	42
V.	The Ethiopian Type in the Fourth Century	67
VI.	The Ethiopian in the Hellenistic World	77
VII.	Terra-Cottas	82
VIII.	Hellenistic Bronzes	92
IX.	New Hellenistic Experiments	101
X.	The Character of the Ethiopian	111
XI.	The Ethiopian in Roman Literature	115
XII.	The Ethiopian in Roman Art	121
	Bibliography	135
	Index	143

ILLUSTRATIONS			TO FACE PAGE
Fig.	1.	Hydria in Vienna	15
Fig.	2.	Pendant for Necklace	19
Fig.	3.	Earring from Cyprus	19
Fig.	4.	Attic Vase in Boston	24
Fig.	5.	Drinking Cup in Boston	26
Fig.	6.	Janiform Vase in Princeton	26
Fig.	7.	Cantharus in the Vatican	28

vii

viii   CONTENTS

                                                    TO FACE
                                                    PAGE

Fig. 8. Negress on Oenochoe in Baltimore......... 28
Fig. 9. Crocodile and Negro................... 38
Fig. 10. Negro Head from Olynthus............. 72
Fig. 11. Negro's Head from Olynthus............ 72
Fig. 12. Side View of Figure 11................ 72
Fig. 13. Bronze Head of an African.............. 75
Fig. 14. Pitcher in Baltimore................... 88
Fig. 15. Negro in Munich..................... 88
Fig. 16. Vase in Munich...................... 91
Fig. 17. Vase in Munich...................... 91
Fig. 18. Bronze Statuette from Carnuntum........ 94
Fig. 19. Bronze Negro Boy.................... 97
Fig. 20. Bronze Ethiopian Boy................. 98
Fig. 21. Agate in Baltimore................... 109
Fig. 22. Clay Vase in Baltimore................ 109
Fig. 23. Ethiopian Slave Cleaning a Boot......... 109
Fig. 24. Marble Head in Berlin................ 132

PREFACE

No barbarian race held as continuous an interest for the
Greek and Roman artist as the Ethiopian. Realistic portraits
of other known races in the classical world are relatively few
and belong usually to the Hellenistic and Roman eras. The
negro, on the other hand, was rendered with the utmost fidelity to the racial type during the most restrained and idealistic
period of Greek art. Attic vase painters who were content to
indicate Orientals by their dress with scarcely any distinguishing marks of race, delineated with marked realism the
woolly hair and thick lips of the Ethiopian. From its earliest
appearance the popularity of the type never waned in any
productive period of classical art.

Due to the humble position of the Ethiopian in Greece and
the fact that realism was usually confined to smaller objects
the great sculptors did not consider him a sufficiently dignified or important subject, since life-sized heads and statues are
comparatively few. But for smaller objects the popularity of
the type was tremendous, and is attested by a wealth of statuettes, vases, engraved gems, coins, lamps, weights, finger-
rings, ear-rings, necklaces and masks from classical sites.

Literary evidence as to the status of the black race in Greek
and Roman life is very slight and to supplement our knowledge one must turn to the art objects which show the type.
Interest was drawn to this problem at the time when the
excitement over the abolition of negro slavery was raging in
the United States prior to the Civil War. The earliest important work on the subject was a monograph entitled *Die
Aethiopen der altclassischen Kunst*, by J. Loewenherz, published in an important year in negro history, 1861. This
monograph does not fulfill the promise of its title, for the
examples in art are subordinated to a study of the Memnon
myth and a discussion of the real and mythical Ethiopian

ix

lands. In 1885 Von Schneider published an article [1] in which he classified chronologically the examples which he knew, and which he later supplemented by a list of examples brought to his attention in the interval.[2] The most important contribution to the subject has recently been made by Buschor in an article entitled *Das Krokodil des Sotades*,[3] which gives a very full account of the negro on vases of the fifth century.

Other work on the question has been confined to the publication of individual specimens which have come into museum or private collections. Sometimes this has been made the basis of a substantial article as in the case of Schrader [4] who compares at great length a head of a Libyan in the British Museum with a head of a negro in Berlin and who assembles some examples of Ethiopians relevant to his discussion. But in the main such articles have done no more than list a few unrelated examples of the type and make some inaccurate generalizations. This is probably due to the fact that only a few of the ancient negro portraits are well known, since only a few have been widely reproduced by illustration. The need for a new and more complete list has been frequently expressed. Wace expressed the hope that this would form a part of Bienkowski's *Corpus Barbarorum*.[5] Von Schneider, who had great interest in the subject, announced his intention of supplementing his list by a more complete study but died without realizing this aim.

At the suggestion of Professor David M. Robinson this study was undertaken. Representations of the negro type have proved to be so common that a complete list is an impossibility, as practically every museum or private collection contains one or more examples. This forces us to depend on catalogues, and as many negro types occur on minor objects

---

[1] *Jb. Kunst. Samml.*, III, 1885, pp. 3 ff.
[2] *Jh. Oest. Arch. Inst.*, IX, 1906, pp. 321-324.
[3] *Muen. Jb. Bild. Kunst*, XI, 1919, pp. 1-43.
[4] *Berlin Winckelmannsprogram*, LX, 1900.
[5] *B. S. A.*, X, 1903-4, p. 108.

they are not always illustrated. But the writer feels that the range of cases here given is sufficiently extended so that the principal types have all been included and she is encouraged by the very incomplete knowledge shown in previous references on the subject. She has visited many European and American museums in her study of the negro but lays no claim to a complete knowledge of all examples. The terminology has been a real difficulty, since the popular and the scientific understanding of the word " negro " are at variance. European usage in this matter is far from uniform and often careless. The German archaeologists use " Neger " and " Mohr " indiscriminately as synonymous, even Buschor in his excellent article employing them in the same sentence. Museum catalogues use one term as frequently as the other and a study of the objects shows that they are not employed to distinguish a Moor from a Sudanese but that the usage is very loose. The French archaeologists use " nègre " to cover all variations of dark skin regardless of the features or hair. This is doubtless because of more frequent contact with France's North African colonies than with those south of the Great Desert. English scholars, more familiar with Egypt, frequently call these classical negroes Nubians, a usage which has considerable warrant in that many entered Greece by way of Egypt from Nubia. The English also employ the word " negro " but the longer term Ethiopian is generally avoided.

Science limits the name " negro " to one group of African races, the Ulotrichi, the determining factor being, not the skin, but the crisply curling so-called woolly hair. The principal representatives of this group are the stock of Senegambia and Guinea, and its other outstanding characteristics are a short, broad nose, thick, projecting lips, a prominent jaw and abnormally long arms. So complicated are the racial and tribal divisions and subdivisions in Africa with their varying characteristics that the classification of the art types according to racial origins is too difficult for the archaeologist. America, with a delicate race problem on her hands, has long since disregarded any scientific distinctions between the various African types, and the popular usage in this country defines a negro in the terms of the color line. Generally speaking racial feeling is directed against skin, and variations of the hair and features are not taken into account. The use of the word is further complicated by existing legal definitions such as that of the State of North Carolina, which declares any person a negro who has in his veins one-sixteenth or more of African blood.

Greek literature has no such confusion in nomenclature and gives very generally to any member of any dark-skinned tribe the name Αἰθίοψ, which the Greek geographers derived from αἴθός and ὄψ that is to say, a man with a (sun) burned face. It is not at all restricted to the kingdom of Meroë south of Egypt. The Greek use of *Aithiops*, therefore, closely parallels the popular use of negro and is quite at variance with its restricted scientific use. To use negro in its scientific sense in the present study would be to exclude many Ethiopians. To defer to popular usage would be unscientific and would cause frequent misunderstandings. Therefore it seems best to retain the Greek word in its English form, *Ethiopian,* and to indicate genuine negro types under the individual descriptions, particularly since this study limits its scope to Ethiopians in Greece and Rome and is not concerned with their original African homes.

My heartiest thanks are due to Professor David M. Robinson who has supervised and assisted in all stages of preparation with that generosity well known to all his students and to Professor Tenney Frank, who read a portion of the manuscript.

THE NEGRO IN GREEK AND ROMAN CIVILIZATION

CHAPTER I

THE ETHIOPIAN IN GREEK LITERATURE

The absence of exact geographical knowledge of Africa and eastern Asia is the basic reason for the profound confusion in the Greek mind about the Ethiopians. Appearing in Homer as the comrades of the Olympic gods, interwoven with the myths of Memnon and Andromeda, emerging actually as persons of curious appearance from the lands south of Egypt, it is small wonder that writers like Strabo and Pausanias found it difficult to reconcile them in geography and legend, and that in different periods they were identified with widely differing peoples.

The confusion begins with Homer himself, to whom Ethiopia was a land at the remotest border of the world beside the stream of Ocean. Here dwelt a blameless race of men who held sacrificial feasts which the gods attended; Zeus and the other gods in *Il.* I, 423-4:

> Ζεὺς γὰρ ἐς Ὠκεανὸν μετ' ἀμύμονας Αἰθιοπῆας
> χθιζὸς ἔβη κατὰ δαῖτα, θεοὶ δ'ἅμα πάντες ἕποντο

Iris in *Il.* XXIII, 205-7:

> οὐχ ἕδος · εἶμι γὰρ αὖτις ἐπ' Ὠκεανοῖο ῥέεθρα,
> Αἰθιόπων ἐς γαῖαν, ὅθι ῥέζουσ' ἑκατόμβας
> ἀθανάτοις, ἵνα δὴ καὶ ἐγὼ μεταδαίσομαι ἱρῶν

and Poseidon in *Od.* I, 22-24:

> 'Αλλ' ὁ μὲν Αἰθίοπας μετεκίαθε τηλόθ' ἐόντας,
> Αἰθίοπας, τοὶ διχθὰ δεδαίαται, ἔσχατοι ἀνδρῶν,
> οἱ μὲν δυσομένου Ὑπερίονος, οἱ δ'ἀνιόντος—

1

2   THE NEGRO IN GREEK AND ROMAN CIVILIZATION

In another passage the Ethiopians were visited by Menelaus, *Od.* IV, 84:

Αἰθίοπας θ'ἱκόμην καὶ Σιδονίους καὶ 'Ερεμβοὺς

They were included in a list of places decidedly near-eastern; and with Homer begins also the conception of the two-fold Ethiopians (cf. *Od.* I, 24 as quoted above), those of the east and the west, of the rising and the setting sun. We are given no clue as to which group of Ethiopians was visited by Zeus in company with the other gods, but Poseidon seems to have visited the eastern Ethiopians, since he was in Asia Minor on his way home when he caught sight of Odysseus on his raft,[1] *Od.* V, 282-3:

Τὸν δ'ἐξ Αἰθιόπων ἀνιὼν κρείων ἐνοσίχθων
τηλόθεν ἐκ Σολύμων ὀρέων ἴδεν·

Iris must have been visiting the Ethiopians of the west since she stops at the palace of Zephyrus on her way. But the western Ethiopians play a minor part in Greek mythology for as the Memnon myth grew in importance, the son of the Dawn who was also king of the Ethiopians, fixed them in the East, where Eos and Tithonus dwelt παρ' 'Ωκεανοῖο ῥοῆς ἐπὶ πείρασι γαίης (*Hymn to Aphrodite*, 228).

The Ethiopians of Homer, ἔσχατοι ἀνδρῶν, comrades of the gods rather than of men, are creatures too shadowy for any description of their personal appearance. There is no indication that they were black, no allusion to the later etymology [2] which derived Ethiopians from αἴθω and ὄψ, that is (sun) burnt faces. On the other hand we can not argue that Homer had never heard of dark men because he does not specifically mention them, and in his linking of the Ethiopians so closely with the rising and the setting of the sun he can not have

---

[1] Cf. Wilamowitz, *Homerische Untersuchungen*, p. 17; Leaf, *Troy, a Study in Homeric Geography*, pp. 309-310.

[2] Cf. Stephanus of Byzantium, *Thesaurus s. v.* Αἰθίοψ; *Etym. Mag. s. v.* Αἰθιοπία; Suidas *s. v.* Αἰθίοψ.

THE ETHIOPIAN IN GREEK LITERATURE 3

been entirely unmindful of the action of the sun's rays. It is not inconceivable to see in the western Ethiopians, who seem to have no other *raison d'être* than to fill a geographical gap, a subconscious reasoning that the sun must color men dark in the region where it sets not less than where it rises. But they are entirely fabulous and any attempt to place them in a fixed geographical scheme is futile, since Homer himself says that we do not know the places where the sun rises and sets, *Od.* X, 190-192 :

> ὦ φίλοι, οὐ γάρ τ'ἴδμεν ὅπη ζόφος οὐδ' ὅπη ἠὼς,
> οὐδ' ὅπη ἠέλιος φαεσίμβροτος εἶσ'ὑπὸ γαῖαν
> οὐδ' ὅπη ἀννεῖται.

Only the Ethiopians visited by Menelaus have a faint ring of reality, as these are listed with actually existing peoples including Egyptians. If we wish to think that Homer had heard vaguely of dark men in the south it proves nothing that Menelaus visited them by ship. Shakspere in an age of greater knowledge gave a sea-coast to Bohemia.

References to Ethiopians in Hesiod are hardly more definite than in Homer. In a fragment quoted by Strabo VII, 3, 7, Hesiod lists Ethiopians with Ligurians and Scythians, people of whom Hesiod could have no very definite knowledge but who are not mythical.[3] Löwenherz (p. 9) is wrong in saying that Hesiod has actual information about African Ethiopians since he names them together with the Libyans. There is no manuscript warrant for reading Libyans here nor any reason for substituting them unless Hesiod shows elsewhere that he knows the real location of Ethiopia. This he does not, for in *Theogony* 984-5 the Ethiopians are without a definite home, and Memnon the son of Eos is their king. Hesiod in the fragment is apparently listing a few tribes who are to him extremely remote, the extremes of north, west and south. Nor is there in Hesiod any specific reference to the Ethiopian

---

[3] Cf. Rzach, *Hesiodi Carmina*, p. 148, frag. 55 Αἰθίοπάς τε Λίγυς τε Σκύθας ἱππημολγούς. The Strabo mss. read Λιγυστί δὲ.

4   THE NEGRO IN GREEK AND ROMAN CIVILIZATION

color, though nameless dark men in the south are referred
to for the first time in the *Works and Days* where (527) it
is said that in winter the sun goes ἐπὶ κυανέων ἀνδρῶν δῆμόν τε
πόλιν τε. In spite of the gloss, Αἰθιόπων-Μαύρων-κυανέων, the
reference here may be to Egyptians, though the adjective
κυανέοισι is later applied to Memnon's Ethiopians by Quintus
of Smyrna, II, 101. In a fragment of Mimnermus (Bergk⁴
12; Diehl 10) the sun goes γαῖαν ἐς Αἰθιόπων ἵνα δὴ θοὸν ἅρμα
καὶ ἵπποι | ἑστᾶσ', ὄφρ' 'Ηὼς ἠριγένεια μόλῃ. The Ethiopians are
again in the East and the western Ethiopians have disappeared, at least for the time being, for Mimnermus evidently
thinks of them as sufficiently fixed in the east to be synonymous with it and sufficiently mythical to be contrasted with
the Hesperides.

Aeschylus is the first Greek writer to place the Ethiopians
definitely in Africa. Prometheus (*Prom.* 808-9) refers to a
dark race, κελαινὸν φῦλον, who dwell near the springs of the
sun where the Ethiopian river is, ποταμὸς Αἰθίοψ. Were it
not for mention of the Nile River and the Egyptians this
would sound like a complete return to the mythical Ethiopians
near the stream of Ocean. The reference to the springs of
the sun and the fact that in the *Suppliants* (280-2) they
were neighbors of the Indians show that Aeschylus' geography
was very inexact. In fact the Ethiopians again recede into a
mythical haze in a fragment (Nauck 192) from the *Prometheus Unbound* of Aeschylus quoted by Strabo, I, 2, 27:

> φοινικόπεδον τ' ἐρυθρᾶς ἱερὸν
> χεῦμα θαλάσσης,
> χαλκοκέραυνόν τε παρ' 'Ωκεανῷ
> λίμναν παντοτρόφον Αἰθιόπων,
> ἵν' ὁ παντόπτας 'Ηλιος αἰεὶ
> χρῶτ' ἀθάνατον κάματόν θ'ἵππων
> θερμαῖς ὕδατος
> μαλακοῦ προχοαῖς ἀναπαύει.

Strabo, who tries hard to reconcile the Ethiopia of Homer

THE ETHIOPIAN IN GREEK LITERATURE 5

and Aeschylus with his own geographical knowledge, explains
this passage by saying that since the stream of Ocean refreshes
the sun along the whole southern belt, Aeschylus appears to
place his Ethiopians along this whole belt. They are probably
also the μελανοτέρφων γένος (Nauck, Aes., Fr. 370) preserved
by the scholiast of Apollonius Rhodius (IV, 1348) who explains that Aeschylus means those whose whole body is dark.

From the vague and unreal Ethiopians of poetry one is
recalled into reality rather sharply by Herodotus' matter-of-
fact description of two sets of Ethiopians who entered Greece
in the army of Xerxes. Herodotus distinguishes sharply
between the straight hair of the Asiatic Ethiopians and the
woolly hair of those from Africa. They are not presented as
corresponding to Homer's twofold Ethiopians, though Homer-
loving Greeks must have considered this a verification of the
poet's geographical knowledge. Herodotus shows himself a
rather superficial observer of racial differences, as he mentions
hair as the only distinguishing mark between the two groups,
although he goes into their costumes and weapons in some
detail.[4] It is significant that nowhere does Herodotus refer
to dark skin, apparently taking this for granted as understood,
and showing that the identification of Ethiopians with the
black races must have dated well before his time.

In view of the fact that Herodotus had discussed the type
scientifically, and that vase painters had familiarized it at
Athens some time before the plays of Euripides were produced, one is surprised to have the Ethiopians again retire to
a mythical landscape on the world's edge as they do in a
fragment of the *Phaethon* of Euripides.[5] But even though
the Ethiopians are again mythical they are by now surely
dark; it is made explicit that Ethiopia, the country implied
by the proper names, is the home of the swarthy race who
daily are the first to be struck by the golden flame of the sun.

---

[4] Cf. Her. VII, 70. For the eastern Ethiopians mentioned by
Herodotus, cf. Macan's note and A. H. Keane, *Ethnology*, C. XI.

[5] Cf. Nauck, Euripides, frag. 771 (quoted by Strabo 1, 2, 27).

2

6   THE NEGRO IN GREEK AND ROMAN CIVILIZATION

The explanation is that the Ethiopians have become a fixed literary tradition in Greek poetry, maintaining a separate life of their own and having little to do with reality. Every literature retains certain supernatural beings who become a part of the poetical heritage of their country and who have a long literary history. This is the reason that no inconsistency was felt when poetry suddenly transplanted the Ethiopians from Africa to the extreme east. It is also the reason why the purely poetical western Ethiopians reappear in the *Argonautica* of Apollonius Rhodius (III, 1190 f.) :

> ἠέλιος μὲν ἄπωθεν ἐρεμνὴν δύετο γαῖαν
> ἑσπέριος, νεάτας ὑπὲρ ἄκριας Αἰθιοπήων

in an age when great numbers of terra-cotta figurines portrayed the negro type with a realism that often amounted to caricature. The Ethiopians of the poets—Homer, Hesiod, Mimnermus, Aeschylus, Euripides, Apollonius—are mythical or partly mythical creatures, while the writers of prose— Herodotus, Strabo, Pliny, Heliodorus—dealt with the African reality.

Whenever the mythical Ethiopians appear in conjunction with definite heroes or heroines of mythology they shrink in importance. Interest is centered in the principal actor and mention of them is purely formal, without additional description, as a part of the hero's title. They are closely associated with Memnon, a hero of the epic cycle, and with the post-Homeric myth of Andromeda, daughter of Cepheus and Cassiopeia.

Memnon [6] does not appear in the *Iliad* but is twice referred to in the *Odyssey*, once (though not by name) as the son of Eos who slew Antilochus (IV, 187-8), and once for his great beauty (XI, 522). It will be noted that Homer does not call

---

[6] Cf. Preller, *Griechische Mythologie*, I, p. 361; II, pp. 435-6; Roscher, *Lexicon der gr. und röm. Myth. s. v.* Memnon; Gruppe, *Gr. Mythologie*, pp. 679-683; Löwenherz, *Die Aethiopen der altclassischen Kunst*, pp. 18-32.

THE ETHIOPIAN IN GREEK LITERATURE   7

him the king of the Ethiopians. He is the beautiful son of
Eos, and as the son of so fair a goddess he would not have
been thought of as dark-skinned. His identification with the
Ethiopians, whether known and not mentioned by Homer or
developed soon after, seems to be a reconciliation of two distinct legends—one which placed a fabulous race of men at the
place where the sun rose, and one which brought a hero son
of Dawn to Troy from the sun-rise regions. It was an easy
step to make the dawn hero the king of the dawn folk or
Ethiopians though the association of the two always puzzled
the Greeks. The practical Romans finally made Memnon
himself an outright Ethiopian.

That Memnon's association with the Ethiopians was com-
pleted before the time of Hesiod is clear, for the Theogony
(984-5) names him their king. The identification must
have been made before or by the *Aithiopis*, an epic poem
assigned to Arctinus of Miletus and lost except for a few
fragments and an echo in the *Posthomerica* of Quintus of
Smyrna. The fragments do not mention Ethiopians. The
central theme of the *Aithiopis*, judging from literary references and vase paintings, was Memnon's participation at Troy
on the Trojan side, his victory over Antilochus the son of
Nestor, his death at the hands of Achilles and the grief of
his mother Eos.[7]

Memnon was originally an eastern or Asiatic hero and
many places in Asia were associated with his name. He was
particularly connected with Persia where he was thought to
have built Susa.[8] But Pausanias says that he went from
Ethiopia to Egypt, then to Susa and from there to Troy.[9]
For other places associated with him, see Letronne.[10] Later
his identification by the Greeks with the so-called " Vocal

---

[7] Cf. Gruppe, *op. cit.*, pp. 679-683; Robert, *Scenen der Ilias und
Aithiopis;* Lung, *Memnon*.

[8] Cf. Her. V, 54; VII, 151; Pausanias, IV, 31, 5.

[9] Paus. I, 42, 3; X, 31, 7.

[10] *La Statue vocale de Memnon*; Löwenherz, *op. cit.*, pp. 24-9.

8   THE NEGRO IN GREEK AND ROMAN CIVILIZATION

Memnon " or statue of Amenophis at Thebes transferred him
to Africa and heightened the mystery of his origin.

Asiatic also was the myth of Andromeda,[11] whose parents
Cepheus and Cassiopeia were rulers of Ethiopia. Through
the command of Ammon she was bound to a rock as a sacrifice
to a sea monster and saved by Perseus, who was returning
from his battle with Medusa. The myth is not an early one
but was well known by the fifth century B. C., where it was
a subject for vase painters and dramatic writers. Sophocles
and Euripides each wrote an *Andromeda.*[12] The Ethiopian
country of the Andromeda legend was also in antiquity a
debated point. The similarity between the names *Iope* and
Ethiopia[13] caused the myth to be localized at Joppa,[14] the
presence of a sea monster demanding a sea-coast country.
Even in the time of Josephus the traces of Andromeda's
fetters were pointed out at Joppa.[15] On the other hand, later
writers believed the scene to be African and Heliodorus[16]
says that Perseus, Andromeda and Memnon were worshipped
as heroes in African Ethiopia.

As Memnon because of his great beauty was evidently white,
and Andromeda is white in vase paintings, the ruling caste
of Ethiopia must have been considered white. But what was
the color of the people ruled over? Greek writers seem to
have avoided this problem by silence and the purely formal
mention as given above. But the vase painter wanting to
portray Memnon or Andromeda was confronted with the
necessity of selecting a physiognomy for their followers or
servants. Hence on certain vases treated in another chapter
negro types appear. And here lies the relevancy of this

---

[11] Cf. Hyginus, *Fab.* 64; Apollodorus, *Bibliotheca*, II, 4, 3.

[12] Cf. Nauck, *op. oit.*, pp. 157 ff. and 392 ff.; Gruppe, *op. oit.*, p.
161; *J. H. S.* XXIV, 1904, pp. 99 ff.

[13] Paus. IV, 35, 9.

[14] *Et. Mag. s. v.* 'Ιόπη.

[15] Cf. Josephus, *Bell. Jud.* III, 9, .

[16] *Aethiopicon*, IV, 8.

THE ETHIOPIAN IN GREEK LITERATURE   9

discussion to the problem of the Ethiopian type in art. For the painters did not create fanciful Ethiopians, but apparently reproduced negro types with which they were well acquainted. Negroes had appeared in Athens. Hence, if the legend specified Ethiopians these were the Ethiopians which the painter knew, and they are interesting more for what they can disclose of contemporary slave life in Greece than for their connection with the myth.

The accuracy of knowledge displayed in regard to the geographical Ethiopia by Greek and Roman authors, their involved grouping of the Ethiopian according to habits of eating and living and their uncertain boundaries, is outside the present question. Some time has been given to the mythical Ethiopians because in the first place they are really Greek, a product of the Greek imagination and a tradition of Greek literature. In the second place, Greek poets created the art interest in the Ethiopian type and gave it a legendary aura which can be held in large measure responsible for the curiosity which prompted the reproduction of the type in Greek art. One can almost see the potter look at his model, as he created one of those joyously realistic plastic heads of negroes, and muse " Can these be the blameless Ethiopians of Homer? "

CHAPTER II

The Introduction of the Ethiopian into Greece

Greek literature gives but little information as to the presence of Ethiopians on Greek soil. From Herodotus [1] we learn that they formed a part of the army of Xerxes which invaded Greece in the year 480 B. C. A casual reference in Theophrastus [2] tells us that it was fashionable to have Ethiopian slave characters in the third century B. C. But the evidence of excavations shows that they were known even in Minoan times.

1. Cf. Evans, *B. S. A.*, VII, 1900-01, p. 26; K. Müller, *Jb. Arch. I*, XXX, 1915, p. 272; Evans, *The Palace of Minos*, I, p. 312, fig. 231; p. 526, fig. 383.

A fragment of a painted stucco relief, found at Cnossus, which shows a man's hand fingering a necklace which has pendants in the form of heads of Ethiopian type with large triple earrings, dates from the period of Middle Minoan III. The hair is black and curly, the eyes large, the noses short and the lips thick and red. The color of the skin is a tawny yellow. From the dull orange beads and yellow faces Evans suggests that the material was gold and believes that a man is putting a necklace about a woman's neck perhaps in a wedding ceremony. Evans says that " the golden material of the necklace, coupled with the negroes' heads, seems to point to Nubia—the Egyptian ' Eldorado ' as the source of the precious metal," but he also thinks it possible that the gold may have come from some other African source south of the desert by way of Libya, as there is other evidence that the Cretans had relations with the Libyans.

2. Cf. *Palace of Minos*, I, pp. 302, 310; figs. 228, c; 230, a, b, and c; II, p. 757, fig. 489.

Faïence fragments found with the so-called Town Mosaic,

---

[1] Her. VII, 69, 70.

[2] Cf. Theophrastus, *Characters*, VII, Jebb., pp. 62-63.

THE INTRODUCTION OF THE ETHIOPIAN INTO GREECE   11

which date perhaps even earlier from Middle Minoan II times, show types which Evans considers negroid from the swarthy skin color, prognathism, and shape of the torso. He believes that they form part of a siege scene and that some are in the attitude of suppliants. To Late Minoan I b, the age of the great expansion overseas, belong the remains of a fresco on which the "Minoan Captain of the Blacks" is leading the negro troops. The employment of negro auxiliaries by Minoan lords is a historical fact of great significance. Perhaps they indicate conquest in Africa where there were caravan routes to the interior of immemorial antiquity. Their employment as Palace Guards and auxiliaries on European soil is paralleled by the use of Senegalese troops in modern warfare.

3. Cf. Evans, *Palace of Minos*, II, pp. 756-7, pl. XIII.

From these Minoan fragments it is evident that the Cretans had some knowledge of dark races in Africa. This knowledge does not seem to have been carried over to the mainland; Mycenean or Helladic art has not afforded any portraits of Ethiopians and it is difficult to believe with Evans that the Minoans made use of black regiments for their final conquest of a large part of the Peloponnese and Mainland Greece. In any case the art type would have died out with the Indo-European invasions. Beyond this Greek literature is silent and the many representations of the negro type in Greek art must furnish their own interpretation.

The earliest appearance of the Ethiopian type in the art of the mainland is on a series of plastic vases in the form of heads, some single and some janiform. Schneider believed that negroes entered Greece for the first time in the army of Xerxes and that their sudden appearance in art is due to the deep impression left in the minds of those who saw them. A glance at these vases convinces one that here is no memory picture. The racial type is rendered with great fidelity. Here is the true negro type, woolly-haired, prognathous, with broad nose and large everted lips. There is no doubt that Ethiopians were actually on Greek soil and that they served as models for

12   THE NEGRO IN GREEK AND ROMAN CIVILIZATION

the potter. These vases from the evidence of their decoration
and shape can now be dated in the latter part of the sixth
century B. C. Consequently Ethiopians did not enter Greece
for the first time in Xerxes' army, and we must look for an
earlier link between Greece and Ethiopia.

The most obvious connection between the two geographically
is Egypt. Here the Ethiopian had been known for centuries,
and had appeared upon Egyptian monuments since the second
Dynasty, roughly corresponding to the Early Minoan period.
There have recently come to the Boston Museum two excellent
painted limestone portraits of an Egyptian Ethiopian prince
and princess dating about 3000 B. C. Dr. Reisner calls these
"the earliest known portraits of negroes," but it has been
wrongly denied that these are negroes by Petrie in *Ancient
Egypt,* 1916, p. 48.

Prior to the founding of Alexandria, the strongest bond
between Egypt and Greece was the city of Naucratis in the
Nile delta. Flinders Petrie (*Naukratis* I, p. 5), and Prinz
(*Funde aus Naukratis,* pp. 1-6) place the date of its founding by Milesian colonists in the early half of the seventh
century B. C. from the evidence of its pottery and scarab
industry, and from the testimony of Greek authors. By the
middle of the sixth century it had achieved a marked commercial eminence. It was granted certain privileges and
immunities by the government of Egypt. It was the gateway
of Egypt for all foreigners, since it was the only port of the
delta which foreign ships were permitted to enter. It was,
therefore, the most logical place for Greeks to have their first
contact with members of the Ethiopian race, and the first
negroes to enter Greece were in all probability brought back
by returning voyagers from Naucratis.

Naucratis was important not only as a commercial but also
as an artistic center, and if we are correct in assuming that
Ethiopians became known to Greece by way of this city, we
should expect them to appear in thee art of Naucratis before
they occur in the art of the mainland. Excavations have

THE INTRODUCTION OF THE ETHIOPIAN INTO GREECE 13

proved this to be the case, and the popularity of the type to have lasted into later centuries. Furthermore the founders of Naucratis were Ionic Greeks from the mainland of Asia Minor and the interrelation between the Ionian art centers in the early period is well established. There is, therefore, additional support for this conjecture in the fact that the Ethiopian type occurs on objects of the seventh and sixth centuries from Cyprus and Rhodes, two islands influenced by the art of Naucratis. Furtwängler (*Griech. Vasenmalerei,* text to pl. 51, pp. 255-260) assigns to an Ionian artist the well known Caeretan hydria depicting the myth of Heracles and Busiris in which Ethiopians are shown as attendants. Karo is of the opinion that the Busiris vase was made in North Africa. Buschor (*Muen. Jb. Bild. Kunst,* XI, p. 36) remarks that the master who painted this hydria must have been familiar with the Naucratite fabric and types. Buschor, however, believes that Ionian artists introduced the negro type into Greek art. This does not contradict the idea that Naucratis played an important part. It only introduces an intermediary step.

The following objects have been found at Naucratis and other places outside the Greek mainland with which Naucratis had trade relations:

VASES

4. London—British Museum—from Naucratis—6th cent. Cf. Petrie, *Naukratis,* I, pl. V, fig. 41, p. 51; Dumont-Chaplain, *Les Céramiques de la Grèce propre;* Walters, *Catalogue of Vases,* II, p. 83, B 102 (33); Buschor, *Mün. Jb. Bild. Kunst,* XI, 1919, p. 35.

This vase fragment shows the figure of an Ethiopian from head to waist. The type is strongly marked; the lips are prominent and everted, the nose short and broad, the hair woolly. The head is in profile but the body and arms are full front. The right arm is held out from the body with the forearm extending downward. The left arm is missing above the elbow but was probably held up in the same posture as in the following figure. The shoulders are very broad and the waist narrow. Lines of white down the front of the chest and at

14   THE NEGRO IN GREEK AND ROMAN CIVILIZATION

the right elbow seem to indicate that the figure is not nude but
is wearing a close-fitting jacket with sleeves. Buschor suggests
that this Ethiopian may be one of the attendants of Busiris
running away before the attack of Heracles, since he considers
that this story originated in Naucratis. It is equally probable
that the pose, which recurs on the two following examples is
a dancing one, since it is identical with the pose of a number
of the revellers on the Fikellura amphora from Samos now
in Altenburg. The revellers although painted in solid black
are not Ethiopian in feature. The design is in black on a drab
ground, with details added in purple and white. Size 2¾
by 2½ in.

5. London—British Museum—from Naucratis—6th cent. Cf.
Petrie, *Naukratis*, I, pl. V, fig. 40; Buschor, *Mün. Jb. Bild.
Kunst*, XI, 1919, p. 35.

This fragment of a vase shows a figure in black on a light
ground similar in pose to the preceding. The face is smaller
and the features are so conventionalized that it is not certain
that an Ethiopian is meant, though the black paint and similarity of pose make it probable.

6. London—British Museum—from Naucratis—6th cent. Cf.
Petrie, *Naukratis*, I, pl. V, fig. 42; Buschor, *Mün. Jb. Bild.
Kunst*, XI, 1919, p. 35.

This fragment of the same ware shows a figure similar to
the foregoing except that the figure is preserved far enough
below the knee to indicate the pose. The face also is conventionalized by the prominence of the jaw, and the black color
indicates an Ethiopian. The figure is balanced on the right
leg, and the left is held in the air as if dancing. White lines
on the body probably indicate a garment. Ht. 1½ in.

Fig. 40 on the same plate of the Naukratis publication has
the same pose but a different profile and may not be meant
for an Ethiopian.

7. Vienna—K. K. Oesterr. Museum—from Caere—6th cent. Cf.
Monumenti, VIII, pls. XVI and XVII; Masner, *Sammlung
antiker Vasen und Terrakotten*, pp. 21-22, 217, pl. II; F. R., pl.
51, pp. 255-261, a complete description and full bibliography.

This black-figured hydria depicts the myth of Heracles

FIGURE 1.
HYDRIA IN VIENNA.
Reproduced from Furtwängler-Reichhold, *Griechische Vasenmalerei*.

THE INTRODUCTION OF THE ETHIOPIAN INTO GREEK ART 15

and Busiris, an Egyptian king who made sacrificial victims of all strangers. According to the legend, Heracles permitted himself to be lead to the altar without any show of resistance, but just as the rites were about to commence, turned on Busiris and his priests and killed them with his club and his bare hands. The hydria represents on one side the scene at the altar, where Heracles is despatching Busiris and the Egyptian priests. The other side shows a body-guard of five Ethiopians marching to the assistance of the prostrate king. The Ethiopians are strongly differentiated in type from the Egyptians. Their hair is very woolly and their jaw structure prominent. They are nude except for loin-cloths about their waists, and they carry hooked clubs. They march forward with much spirit and the painter has succeeded in making them life-like and comic. There are no livelier Ethiopians in Greek art. Cf. Fig. 1.

8. Berlin—Antiquarium Inv. 3250—formerly from Cyprus. In Van Branteghem Coll. Froehner, Catal., no. 238; Ohnefalsch-Richter, Kypros, Bibel und Homer, pl. XCIII, 3; p. 216 3; Furtwängler, Arch. Anz., VIII, 1893, pp. 82-83; Prinz, Funde aus Naukratis, p. 105; Buschor, Mün. Jb. Bild. Kunst, XI, 1919, p. 34, fig. 49.

This ointment vase of faience in the form of two conjoined heads represents ethnographic types, one a bearded barbarian and the other a negro with a smooth face. The latter has a broad flat nose and thick lips. His woolly hair is indicated by squares blocked out in the faïence. The vase dates from the seventh century and was made at Naucratis, though found in the Larnaca district on Cyprus.

9. London—British Museum Inv. A 1233—from Cyprus. Cf. Buschor, Mün. Jb. Bild. Kunst, XI, 1919, p. 34, fig. 50.

This janiform ointment vase is similar to the foregoing though differing in the treatment of the Ethiopian's hair. Instead of being blocked out in squares as on the Berlin vase, it is indicated by lozenge-shaped incisions with a dot in the center of each. From the same factory as Nos. 8 and 9 is

16   THE NEGRO IN GREEK AND ROMAN CIVILIZATION

probably *Arch. Anzeiger,* 1928, pp. 77 ff., figs. 1 and 2. Cf. below p. 38. Also to the sixth century belongs the oenochoe from Athens in the form of a single negro head with high handle in the Metropolitan Museum (G. R. 570). The hair is indicated by rough dots in light color, the rest black.

TERRA-COTTAS

10. London—British Museum—from Camirus, Rhodes. Cf. *Synopsis of the Contents of the British Museum, Guide to the 2nd Vase Room,* pt. 2, 1878, p. 10, 68; Walters, *Catalogue of Terracottas,* p. 118, B 269; Winter, *Terrakotten,* II, p. 449, 1 A.

This figurine of terra-cotta is seated in a crouching position, his right leg drawn up in front of him and his left leg drawn under him. His hands clasp his right knee and his chin rests on them. He has thick, negro-like lips, but his ears are those of a satyr. Ht. 4⅛ in.

11. London—British Museum—from Camirus. Cf. *Synopsis, Guide to 2nd Vase Room,* pt. 2, p. 10, 63; Walters, *Terracottas,* p. 118, B. 270; Winter, *Terrakotten,* II, p. 449, 1 b.

This terra-cotta figurine of an Ethiopian is seated in a similar position, except that both legs are drawn up in front. Traces of red color remain. Ht. 4½ in.

12. London—British Museum—from Camirus. Cf. *Synopsis, Guide to 2nd Vase Room,* pt. 2, p. 10, 64; Winter, *Terrakotten,* II, p. 449, 1 b; Walters, *Terracottas,* p. 118, B 271.

Similar figurine of an Ethiopian. Ht. 4½ in.

13. London—British Museum—from Camirus. Cf. *Synopsis, Guide to 2nd Vase Room,* pt. 2, p. 10, 65; Walters, *Terracottas,* p. 118; B 272; Winter, *Terrakotten,* II, p. 449, 1 b.

Similar terra-cotta figurine of an Ethiopian. The right foot is broken off. Ht. 3⅞ in.

14. London—British Museum—from Camirus. Cf. *Synopsis, Guide to 2nd Vase Room,* pt. 2, p. 10, 66; Walters, *Terracottas,* p. 118, B 273; Winter, *Terrakotten,* II, p. 449, 1 b.

Similar terra-cotta figurine. Ht. 3⅞ in.

15. London—British Museum—from Camirus. Cf. *Synopsis, Guide to 2nd Vase Room,* pt. 2, p. 10, 67; Winter, *Terrakotten,* II, p. 449, I B; Walters, *Terracottas,* p. 118, B 274.

Terra-cotta figurine of an Ethiopian, similar in pose to no. 10. Ht. 4¼ in.

THE INTRODUCTION OF THE ETHIOPIAN INTO GREECE   17

16. New York—Metropolitan Museum—Cesnola Coll.—from Cyprus.
Cf. *Atlas of the Cesnola Coll.*, pl. LXXXII, 739; Myres,
Handbook of the Cesnola Coll., p. 362, no. 2320; Winter, *Terrakotten*, II, p. 449, 1 C.

This terra-cotta figurine of an Ethiopian is seated with his right leg drawn up in front of him and his left leg drawn under him. The modelling is crude and the features are indistinct, but the broad nose and thick lips can be distinguished. The eyes are closed. There are remains of a red color on the surface. In type the figure belongs to the series found at Camirus. Ht. 0.09 m.

17. Paris—Louvre—from the Cyrenaica. Cf. Heuzey, *Figurines Antiques de Terre Cuite*, p. 30, pl. 55, 6; Winter, *Terrakotten*, II, p. 449, 1.

This is a terra-cotta figurine of an Ethiopian, similar to the figures from Camirus in the British Museum. The forehead is low, the lips large. Though found in the Cyrenaica, it undoubtedly belongs to the same series. The face is apelike in expression. Ht. 0.09 m.

MINOR OBJECTS

18. Berlin. Cf. Furtwängler, *Aigina*, I, p. 433, no. 19; Buschor, *Mün. Jb. Bild. Kunst*, XI, 1919, p. 34.

Paste scarabaeus of Naucratite fabric with an Ethiopian head in high relief. It is not unnatural to find an object imported from Naucratis in Aegina, a city of commercial enterprise in the early period.

19. London—British Museum—from Naucratis. Cf. Petrie, *Naukratis*, II, pl. XVIII, 35; Buschor, *Mün. Jb. Bild. Kunst*, XI, 1919, p. 34.

Scarabaeus of paste with a negro's head in high relief. The lips are very full, the nose short and flat.

20. London—British Museum—from Naucratis.. Cf. Petrie, *Naukratis*, II, pl. XVIII, no. 61; Buschor, *Mün. Jb. Bild. Kunst*, XI, 1919, p. 34.

Paste scarabaeus similar to the foregoing.

18   THE NEGRO IN GREEK AND ROMAN CIVILIZATION

21. London—British Museum—from Naucratis. Cf. Petrie, *Nau-kratis*, I, pl. XXXVII, nos. 4, 9, 11, 26, 83, 133, 141, 142; pl. XXXVII, 8, 9, 10; II, pl. XVIII, 59, 60; Buschor, *Mün. Jb. Bild. Kunst*, XI, 1919, p. 34.

Scarabaei of paste with the design of a human head. Buschor considers that they represent Ethiopians. This is probable, though the crudity of the work makes it hard to determine. The majority have the reverse design of a winged animal.

22. London—British Museum—from Naucratis. Cf. Walters, *Terracottas*, p. 443, E 91.

Mould for the front of a paste scarab. The design is the head of a negro with a grinning expression. Diam. 1⅛ in.

23. London—British Museum—from Tyre. Cf. *Jb. Arch. I*, II, 1887, p. 197.

Steatite in the form of a scarabaeus, the convex side a negro's head. The flat under-surface has a geometric pattern.

24. Munich—Arndt Coll.—from Cyprus. Cf. Buschor, *Mün. Jb. Bild. Kunst*, XI, 1919, p. 34, fig. 51.

Head of an Ethiopian carved from steatite, the features similar to those of a steatite pendant in the Metropolitan Museum. This head, however, is carved in high relief in the center of a flat oval surface of steatite. The hair is indicated by raised dots. According to Buschor it was used as a seal.

25. Munich—Arndt Coll.—from Cyprus. Cf. Buschor, *Mün. Jb. Bild. Kunst*, XI, 1919, p. 34, fig. 52.

Steatite head of an Ethiopian, smaller than the foregoing. It is carved in high relief from a depression in the center of a flat, round surface. The hair is shown by means of raised dots. The expression is similar to the Ethiopian head on the ear-ring in the Metropolitan Museum, though the features are not as coarse.

26. New York—Metropolitan Museum—Cesnola Coll.—from Cyprus. Cf. Myres, *Handbook of the Cesnola Coll.*, p. 271, no. 1550; *Atlas of the Cesnola Coll.* III, CXV, 2.

Head of a negro carved from steatite. It was intended to be worn as a pendant on a necklace, as it is pierced through above the ears and is flat at the back where it would lie

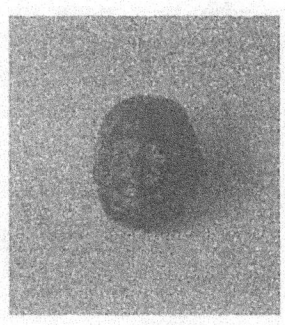

FIGURE 2.

PENDANT FOR NECKLACE. SIXTH CENTURY B. C.

Metropolitan Museum of Art.

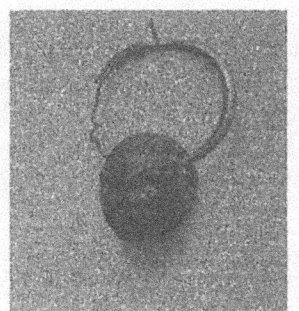

FIGURE 3.

SIXTH CENTURY EARRING FROM CYPRUS.

Metropolitan Museum of Art.

THE INTRODUCTION OF THE ETHIOPIAN INTO GREECE   19

against the neck. The profile is ape-like because of the prominence of the jaw and the low retreating forehead. The nose
is very broad and flat, and the lips wide. The hair is indicated as woolly by a series of drilled holes. Ht. 1½ in. Fig. 2.

27. New York—Metropolitan Museum—Cesnola Coll.—from Cyprus.
   Cf. Myres, *Handbook of the Cesnola Coll.*, p. 380, no. 3161.

Negro head, carved from steatite, as pendant on a gold ear-
ring. It is similar in type to the foregoing, but resembles
an animal in the exaggeration of the features. The curly hair
is indicated by lozenge-shaped incisions similar to those on
an ointment vase in the British Museum. A novel feature is
that the eye-balls are painted red. Fig. 3.

28. Naucratis, Bulak Museum. Cf. Petrie, *Naukratis*, I, p. 43.

Small head of an Ethiopian of dark blue glass, found in
the remains of a private house.

29. London—British Museum—from Cyprus. Cf. Marshall, *Catalogue of Jewellery*, p. 14, 144, fig. 2.

A thin strip of gold embossed with rosettes and conventionalized animal heads. In the center of the strip at the
top is the mask of an Ethiopian on its side. The strip was
found in a Bronze Age tomb in the Larnaca district where
the janiform vase of faïence was found, and is probably one
of the earliest instances outside of Egypt. Length 16.1 cm.

At first glance it seems difficult to generalize about objects
which have so little uniformity. Naucratis may have introduced the type but its adaptations varied widely. A study of
the objects reveals certain general facts. In the art of Naucratis the type occurs on vases and scarabaei. On the island
of Rhodes it was adapted to small terra-cotta figurines. On
Cyprus it was used as the subject of a series of black steatite
heads. On Cyprus were found the two janiform ointment
vases, but these belong to Naucratis, and the Caeretan hydria
is affiliated with Naucratis. The explanation seems to be that
in this early art of Cyprus and Rhodes the Ethiopian was
considered apotropaic, while in Naucratis his apotropaic func-

20   THE NEGRO IN GREEK AND ROMAN CIVILIZATION

tion was giving way to interest in him as an ethnographic type.

The small objects upon which the negro type is found have long been recognized as prophylactic. Two of the steatite heads, and the pendants of the Minoan necklace were obviously intended to be worn as ornaments. Now the tendency to wear or carry about on the person some small object to counteract the evil eye, ward off harm or bring good luck to the wearer is universally found. The steatite and glass heads, paste scarabaei and the gold strip ornamented with the Ethiopian mask are undoubtedly apotropaic in function. This is the reason that the negro head is always in full front, never in profile. This is the reason that the ugliness of the features has beeen exaggerated. The red eye-balls of the small head on the earring are repulsive and the jaw is so prominent that it seems fairly to represent an animal.

The recurrence of the type on later Greek jewelry has caused the frequent generalization that the negro in Greek art was always prophylactic. This is not true of all periods and types of objects. The Attic artists with characteristic delicacy invested the racial type with a spirit which amounts almost to charm. Ugliness of feature was never stressed. Rather they intrigued the Attic artist because of their strange and novel physiognomy, and their reminiscent association with legendary Ethiopia. But in these earlier centuries of greater superstition and lesser knowledge the small objects with the Ethiopian type are without question prophylactic.

To ward off evil influences was probably also the purpose of the terra-cotta figurines from Camirus. These small figures were all found in graves possibly with the intention of providing dead men with a slave in the next world and were certainly to keep away all harm. All the figurines show practically the same pose. The slave crouches on the ground with one or both legs drawn up in front of him. He rests his head on his hands, which clasped about his knee, and his eyes are closed as if in sleep. Probably they do not simulate

THE INTRODUCTION OF THE ETHIOPIAN INTO GREECE 21

death, as the pose recurs on objects of the fifth century and the Hellenistic period which have no funerary purpose. An inscribed gem of the fifth century, now in the Corneto Museum, shows a crouching Ethiopian as the attendant of a youth who is vigorously pouring oil upon himself after some gymnastic exercises. Several early gems show the sleeping slave alone. The pose is common in statuettes of bronze as well as of terra-cotta from the Alexandrian era, one example even showing an Ethiopian street-hawker asleep in this position, with a tray of fruit in front of him and a pet monkey on his shoulder. Schneider dismisses the question with the remark that the pose was a favorite one for slaves in antiquity. While this statement seems to have been deduced from the frequent occurrence of the figurines rather than to explain them, the pose of the Camirus figurines probably has no special significance. It is a posture regularly found among races accustomed to squatting down on the earth. It was also easier to model a terra-cotta figure seated on a somewhat triangular base which supported the figure than to balance a standing figure in a fragile material.

At Naucratis the Ethiopian slave was better known than on Cyprus or Rhodes. If the Greeks there found him sufficiently ugly to be prophylactic, as evidenced by the many scarabaei, they also found him interesting as a type. It would be absurd to call the Ethiopian of the vase fragments and the Caeretan hydria prophylactic. They are the product of a joyous, almost child-like interest in a new race. The negro perhaps unfortunately has always appealed to the comic side of the Caucasian. The negro's propensity to quick laughter, his feeling for music and the dramatic and his loose-jointed dancing have always made him a popular comedian. We know from Hellenistic objects with the negro type that these characteristics have changed no more than the physiognomy, and the Greeks of Naucratis probably enjoyed them fully as much as we do. The figures on the fragments with their exaggerated eyes and queer jackets are undoubtedly

3

22   THE NEGRO IN GREEK AND ROMAN CIVILIZATION

meant to be comic whether they are dancers or whether they
are servants of Busiris running in terror from the onslaughts
of Heracles.   The artist of the Caeretan hydria is openly
inviting laughter at his row of Ethiopian fighters marching
with clumsy weapons to a contest already settled.

An interest in the Ethiopian features more scientific than
humorous is shown by the makers of the ointment vases in
which an Ethiopian is contrasted with an Asiatic.   Whether
or not these faces were intended as an advertisement of the
country from which the perfume came, the intention here was
fairly serious and the matter of setting off one type against
another presented a very neat problem to the potter.   These
vases are extremely significant in that they are the link
between the art of Naucratis and that of the mainland.   The
Attic artist who was the first to portray the Ethiopian type
adopted the medium of the janiform ointment vase.

CHAPTER III

THE FIFTH CENTURY—THE ETHIOPIAN TYPE ON PLASTIC VASES

The Ethiopian type in the art of the mainland first appears, as has been said, on plastic ointment vases in the form of heads. These occur singly or conjoined and the type is not confined to ointment vases, being found on drinking cups and pitchers as well.

OINTMENT VASES

30. Athens—National Museum 2056—from the Cabirium. Cf. Nicole, *Catalogue des Vases Peints*, p. 283.

Plastic ointment vase in the form of the conjoined heads of a cantharus (*Mün. Jb. Bild. Kunst*, XI, 1919, p. 15), but the description given by Nicole, who calls it a balsamaire, specifies the spout and vertical handles of an ointment vase. Nicole states that the type of the Ethiopian is identical with that of the following vase with the love name Leagrus.

31. Athens—National Museum 2160—from Eretria. Cf. Hartwig, 'Αρχ. 'Εφ. 1894, pp. 121-128, pl. 6; Klein, *Griechischen Vasen mit Lieblingsinschriften*, p. 81, 45; Nicole, *Catalogue des Vases Peints*, p. 283, 1227; Ducati, *Storia della ceramica Greca*, II, p. 516, fig. 389.

Ointment vase with cylindrical spout supported by vertical handles, in the form of a head. Perfectly preserved, it is one of the finest examples of the type. The inscription reads Λέαγρος καλός. The hair is indicated by raised dots of clay. Hair, lips and eye-balls are in the color of the clay. The outlines of iris and pupil are indicated by incised lines. The nose is too sharp for the typical Ethiopian nose. Diameter of the base 0.04 m., Ht. 0.28 m.

32. Athens—National Museum 11725. Cf. Nicole, *Catalogue des Vases Peints*, p. 283, 1228.

Ethiopian's head of same type as above. There are traces of an illegible inscription at the top. The eyes are painted white and the iris red. Ht. 0.12 m.

23

24   THE NEGRO IN GREEK AND ROMAN CIVILIZATION

33. Berlin—Antiquarium—Sabouroff Coll.—from Attica. Cf. Furtwängler, *Beschreibung der Vasensamml.*, II, p. 1027, no.
4049; Schrader, *Berliner Winckelm. Program*, VI, 1900, p.
11 and pp. 34-5.

Ointment vase with a cylindrical mouth and two vertical
handles above head. The hair is rendered by raised dots of
clay, which are unpainted. The forehead is wrinkled. The
skin was painted black, leaving the lips in the red color of
the clay. There are traces of white on the eye-ball. The
face has a lively expression. Ht. 0.105 m.

34. Berlin—Antiquarium. Cf. Furtwängler, *Beschreibung der Vasensammlung*, II, p. 784, no. 2757.

Vase with a lecythus mouth over an Ethiopian's head. The
hair was indicated in the clay and painted. Lips and eyes
were left unpainted. Furtwaengler assigns the vase to the
latter half of the fifth century. Ht. 0.115 m.

35. Boston—Museum of Fine Arts, 97089. Cf. *Arch. Anz.*, XIV,
1899, p. 145, no. 55; Buschor, *Mün. Jb. Bild. Kunst*, XI,
1919, p. 10, pl. IV.

Janiform ointment vase. Both heads are Ethiopians made
from the same mould. The forehead is low and retreating,
the nose short and flat and the lips thick and protruding.
The hair is rendered by raised dots in the clay. The flesh is
painted black, but the hair and lips are left in the original
clay color for contrast. White paint is applied to the eye-
balls, and the pupils are painted black. The vase is referred
to as having a " lecythus mouth " in the notice in the *Arch.
Anz.* cited above. Figs. 4a and 4b.

36. London—British Museum. Cf. Walters, *History of Ancient Pottery*, I, pl. XLVI, 2; Buschor, *Mün. Jb. Bild. Kunst*, XI,
1919, p. 10.

Janiform ointment vase combining the heads of an Ethiopian and a Greek girl. The profile of the Ethiopian shows
the sloping forehead, flat nose, thick lips and prominent jaw
of the Boston vase. The Greek girl wears a cap upon which
is painted a wreath of ivy leaves, and below it her hair is indicated by three rows of raised dots. The heads have been
joined less gracefully than on the Boston vase or the Morgan

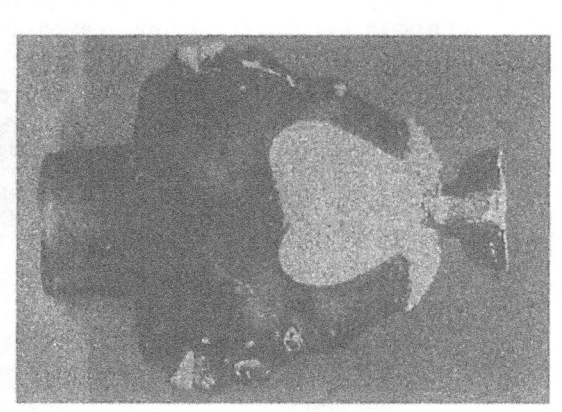

FIGURE 4a.
ATTIC VASE.
In Boston.

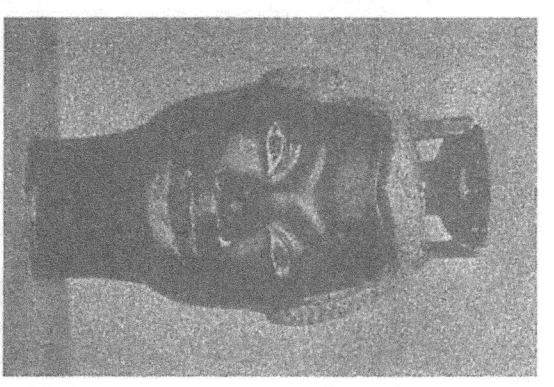

FIGURE 4b.
ATTIC VASE.
In Boston.

THE ETHIOPIAN TYPE ON PLASTIC VASES 25

vase (45). They are telescoped so that they have a single ear between them and the proportions are less pleasing.

37. Paris—Louvre. Cf. Pottier, *Mon. Piot*, IX, 1903, pls. XI and XII; Herford, *Handbook of Greek Vase Painting*, pp. 10 and 80, pl. 2, fig. a; Buschor, *Mün. Jb. Bild. Kunst*, XI, 1919, p. 10.

Janiform ointment vase combining the heads of a negro or negress and a Greek girl. The Ethiopian's profile is identical with that of the Boston and London vases above. The Ethiopian's eyes are almond-shaped and set wide apart. The girl wears a cap painted black on which is a red-figured design of palmettes and cocks. On either side of the girl's neck, running from edge of cap to base, is the inscription καλός written backward.

38. ?—from Calabria. Cf. *Not. Scav.*, 1912, suppl. p. 16, fig. 20; Buschor, *Mün. Jb. Bild. Kunst*, XI, 1919, p. 10.

Ointment vase with a cylindrical spout in the form of an Ethiopian's head. The profile is very different from the Boston, London, and Paris vases. The nose is too long and pointed to be the characteristic Ethiopian's nose. The hair, however, is rendered similarly by raised dots of clay and the flesh is painted black. The lips are thick and protruding. Very lifelike. Red lips and white eyeballs.

DRINKING CUPS

39. Bologna Museum—from the Carthusian Monastery—Certosa. Ht. 0.16 m. Cf. *Bulletino*, 1872, p. 83, no. 36; Buschor, *Mün. Jb. Bild. Kunst*, XI, 1919, pp. 14-15; Seltman, *A. J. A.*, XXIV, 1920, p. 15; Pellegrini, *Museo Civico di Bologna*, pp. 211, 466, figs. 131 and 132; Brunn, *Abh. Mün. Akad.*, XVIII, 1888, p. 168; Zannoni, *Scavi d. C.*, p. 333, pl. LXXXX, n. 6, 14.

Janiform vase, one head a white woman, the other an Ethiopian. The hair of the white woman is in rows of raised dots in the Procles technique. There is a wreath of ivy partly on her cap and partly on the mouth of the vase. The eyes are long and narrow, the lips archaic.

The Ethiopian is from the Charinus mould (p. 32). The hair was left in the color of the clay, but there are traces of brown color on the lips and eyes.

26 THE NEGRO IN GREEK AND ROMAN CIVILIZATION

40. Boston—Museum of Fine Arts. Cf. *Arch. Anz.*, 1899, p. 144, no. 35; Buschor, *Mün. Jb. Bild. Kunst*, XI, 1919, p. 14.

Cantharus in the form of the conjoined heads of an Ethiopian woman and a white girl. There is a band at the top decorated with palmettes in black on a white ground. Under it is the inscription ὁ παῖς καλός. Ht. 0.192 m.

41. Boston—Museum of Fine Arts 9679. Cf. Buschor, *Greek Vase Painting*, p. 120, fig. 101; Buschor, *Mün. Jb. Bild. Kunst*, XI, 1919, p. 13, fig. 19; *Arch. Anz.* XVI, 1901, p. 166.

Drinking cup with one handle in the form of a negro's head, surmounted by a large round vase mouth. The wide band is painted in the black-figured technique, showing the vase to be one of the earliest of the drinking-cup group. The single handle extends from the rim of the cup to the back of the plastic head.

The hair is shown by the familiar raised dots which are left in the color of the clay. In the clay color also are the eyebrows and the thick, protruding lips. The details are painted in with elaborate care and give the combination of black-figured and red-figured head a striking appearance. The wrinkles in the forehead have been incised in the clay and those in the corner of the eyes have been added in white paint. The eye-balls have been painted a staring white and the pupils black. The surface of the skin is a glossy black. Fig. 5.

42. Frankfurt—Hist. Mus., formerly in Bourguignon Coll. Ht. 0.20 m., Diam. 0.115 m. Cf. Schaal, *Griech. Vasen aus Frankfurter Sammlungen*, pl. 49; F. R. Text III, p. 93.

Vase in the form of a negro's head with a cup mouth with a band of red-figured painting showing satyrs. Facial type quite distinct from other heads; Greek, more cylindrical and stiff. Outline of hair different, though left in the color of the clay and not indicated by clay dots or rings. The band of red-figured painting shows a satyr of heavier build than those of Sotades. Eyes and lips are unpainted, the rest is varnished black. One-handled drinking cup. Eyebrows raised, forehead concave and does not slope, nose longer, in line with eyes. Flesh part black. Traces of red and white

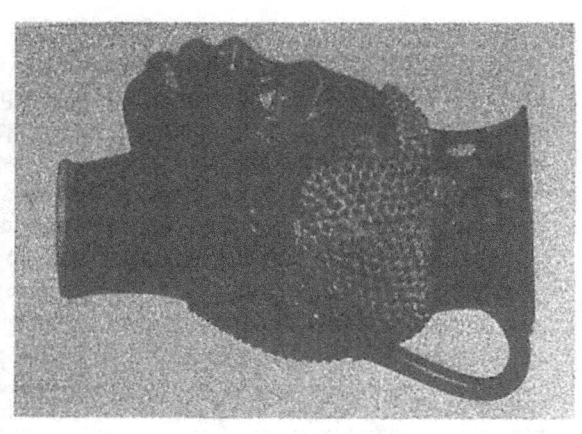

FIGURE 5.
DRINKING CUP.
In the Boston Museum of Fine Arts.

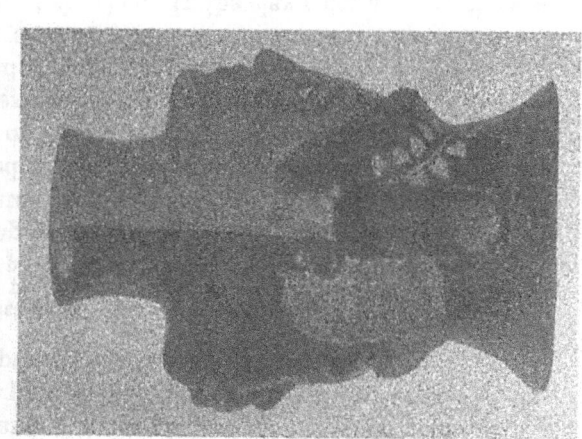

FIGURE 6.
JANIFORM VASE.
In Collection of Mrs. Junius Morgan, Princeton, N. J.

THE ETHIOPIAN TYPE ON PLASTIC VASES 27

color on hair, lips, and eye-balls. Schaal thinks that this is
an excellent portrait, but evidently does not know other good
examples.

The Frankfurt vase has the peculiarity of a hole in the
mouth through which wine could be poured. Schaal suggests
that this may have been intended to create some sport.

43. Greau Collection. Cf. Buschor, *Mün. Jb. Bild. Kunst*, XI,
1919, p. 13; Froehner, *Terrescuites*, 101, pl. V.

Drinking cup with one handle in the form of an Ethiopian's head, dated by Buschor at about the beginning of the
fifth century.

44. Leningrad—Hermitage—no. 836. Cf. Buschor, *Mün. Jb. Bild.
Kunst*, XI, 1919, p. 14.

Janiform cantharus with the heads of an Ethiopian and a
white girl.

45. Princeton—Mus. Coll. of Junius Morgan. Cf. *Art and Archaeology*, XX, 1925, p. 120.

Drinking cup in the form of the conjoined heads of a white
girl and an Ethiopian, both from the Charinus mould. The
white girl is identical with the signed vase of Charinus in
the Corneto Museum. The negro profile is one of the series
identified by the signed fragments in the Villa Giulia
Museum. The white girl wears a cap decorated with an ivy
pattern. The cup mouth is plain. This appears to be a
replica of the vase in Bologna. Fig. 6.

46. Rome—Villa Giulia Museum—from Vignarello. Cf. Della Seta,
Museo di Villa Giulia, I, p. 111, no. 26026; Hoppin, *Handbook of Black-figured Vases*, pp. 72-3.

Fragments of a drinking cup in the form of an Ethiopian's
head. They consist of a part of the cup mouth, two pieces
showing ears and two pieces of a black painted band, one of
which bears the inscription. The decoration of the cup mouth
is identical with that of the Charinus cup in the Corneto
Museum. There is no question that these are fragments of a
negro's head. Fragments of both ears show that they were
painted black, and the hair around them is in raised dots

28   THE NEGRO IN GREEK AND ROMAN CIVILIZATION

left in the color of the clay. Even the shape of the ear is
identical with the Morgan vase.

47. Rome—Vatican—Museo Gregoriano Etrusco. Cf. *Museo Greg.*,
II, pl. LXXXIX; Helbig, *Fuehrer*, ed. 1912, I, p. 326, no.
532; Buschor, *Mün. Jb. Bild. Kunst*, XI, 1919, p. 15; Pottier, *Monuments Piot*, IX, pp. 138 ff.

Janiform cantharus which combines a head of Heracles
with a negro's head. Helbig suggests that the Ethiopian may
be intended for Busiris because he is contrasted with Heracles.
This seems unlikely, since the head of Heracles is also found
in combination with the girl who so often forms the other
half of the janiform Ethiopian vases. As Ridder suggests,
the other head is Omphale. Fig. 7.

48. St. Louis—Museum of Fine Arts. Cf. Furtwängler, *Sitz. Mün.
Akad.*, 1905, p. 243, no. 8; Buschor, *Mün. Jb. Bild. Kunst*, XI,
1919, p. 14, n. 5.

Cantharus in the form of the head of an Ethiopian woman.
She wears a cap. The flesh is painted black, leaving the lips
in the red color of the clay. The teeth are shown and are
painted white, recalling the oenochoe in the collection of Prof.
D. M. Robinson (189). The hair is indicated by wavy, incised
lines instead of the usual raised dots. Eyes and eye-brows are
painted. Myrtle branch on the cup mouth.

49. Vienna — K. K. Oest. Mus. — Castellani Coll. Cf. Brunn,
Bullettino, 1865, p. 241; Schneider, *Jb. Kunst. Samml.*, III,
1885, p. 7, n. 5; Masner, *Sammlung Antiker Vasen*, p. 55, no.
347, pl. VIII.

Cantharus with a band at the top ornamented with palmettes in the red-figured technique. The lower part is the
head of a negress (Masner does not say a woman) wearing a
cap, under the front of which appear a few rows of raised
dots to indicate hair (Procles technique). Prominent jaw,
broad nose, high cheek bones, thick lips. The work has been
carefully done. The flesh is painted black, leaving hair, eye-
brows and lips in the red color of the clay. The eye-balls are
painted white and the teeth show white between the large,
protruding lips. Pupil and iris are marked by incised circles.
Behind the head is a broad red band decorated with white

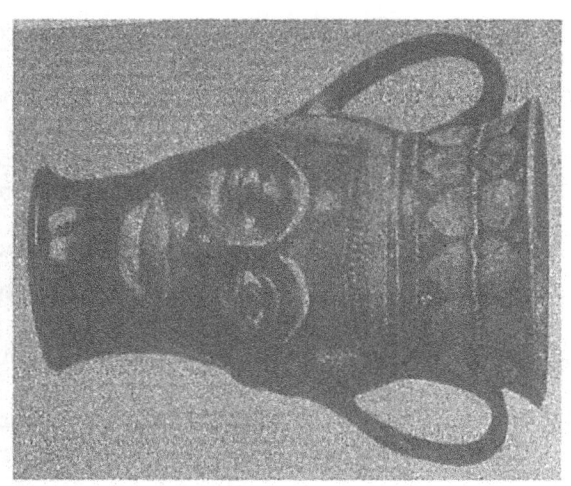

FIGURE 7.
CANTHARUS.
In the Vatican.

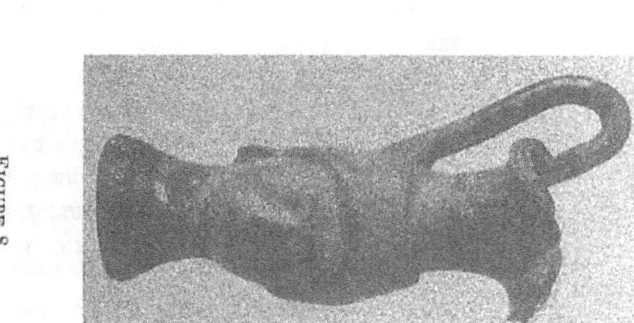

FIGURE 8.
HEAD OF NEGRESS ON OENOCHOE.
In Collection of David M. Robinson, Baltimore, Md.

borders and dots. The ear is modelled with a rosette earring out of a lump of clay. Excellent and careful work of the severe style. Ht. 0.178 m.

50. —from Etruria. Cf. *Bullettino*, 1866, p. 236; Seltman, *A. J. A.*, XXIV, 1920, pp. 14-15.

Janiform cantharus with the conjoined heads of a white girl and an Ethiopian woman. The face of the white girl is pale and somewhat archaic in type. Above both heads is the inscription ὁ παῖς καλός ναί.

PITCHERS—SINGLE HEADS

51. Berlin — Antiquarium — Sabouroff Coll. Cf. Furtwängler, *Beschreibung der Vasensammlung*, II, p. 515, no. 2203; Buschor, *Mün. Jb. Bild. Kunst*, XI, 1919, p. 12 and p. 42, fig. 59.

Oenochoe in the form of a negro's head. The flesh is painted black. The lips and hair, which is indicated by raised dots, are left in the original color of the clay. Ht. 0.17 m.

52. Berlin — Antiquarium — from Athens. Cf. Furtwängler, *Beschreibung der Vasensammlung*, II, p. 515, no. 2204.

Oenochoe similar to the above. The work is more careless. The mouth of the vase is broken off. Ht. 0.07 m.

53. Brussels—Branteghem Coll. Cf. Pottier, *Mon. Piot.* IX, 1903, p. 153, n. 2; Buschor, *Mün. Jb. Bild. Kunst*, XI, 1919, pp. 11-12, fig. 15.

Janiform oenochoe with trefoil top showing the conjoined head of a girl and an Ethiopian. The latter seems in this instance intended to represent a woman since only a band of raised dots indicating hair is shown, back of which is a cap painted black and decorated by a wreath of ivy leaves.

54. Baltimore—Coll. of D. M. Robinson. Cf. Seltman, *A. J. A.*, XXIV, 1920, pp. 14-18.

Oenochoe combining a bearded male head with the head of an Ethiopian woman. Most of the color is gone from the vase and the work is poorer than that of the other known vases of the type. The vase mouth is stocky and not graceful. Attic vase of first half of fifth century B. C. Greatest height, 0.18 m.; of face, 0.045 m. Width of face, 0.04 m. Fig. 8.

30   THE NEGRO IN GREEK AND ROMAN CIVILIZATION

55. Naples—National Museum. Cf. Heydemann, *Vasensammlungen des Museo Nazionale*, p. 447, no. 2950 (Photo Sommer 11079); Buschor, *Mün. Jb. Bild. Kunst*, XI, 1919, p. 12.

Oenochoe in the form of a negro's head. Ht. 0.15 m.

56. —from Svessola—Italian imitation? Cf. *Not. Scav.*, 1878, pl. V, no. 8, p. 397; Buschor, *Mün. Jb. Bild. K.*, XI, 1919, p. 12.

Vase in the form of an Ethiopian's head. Enough of the mouth remains to show that it was probably an oenochoe. The head is covered by raised dots of clay. Forehead is sloping, eyebrows prominent, nose broad though pointed, lips thick and everted.

It was on the ointment vase, as Buschor points out, that the Ethiopian first appeared conjoined with another head in the art of Naucratis in the 7th century. And it is on the ointment vase of the sixth that it was first shown by the Attic potters. This vase form always gave the potter the greatest opportunity for display of individuality in treatment. It needed only a narrow mouth and small handles and lent itself to variety and innovation. Since its shape was not prescribed it was the starting point for novelties of design which eventually influenced other vase forms as well.

The Attic ointment vases in the form of double heads show a profound advance over those of Naucratis. The funnel-shaped vase mouth and vertical handles, while they are the same type, have been refined. The mouth rests on a more slender cylindrical neck and the handles which support its edge are less clumsy. They now rise from the side of the head instead of from the hair above the center of the forehead. The ointment vase type from Naucratis had little grace, since the chins of the two heads were enlarged and extended to meet and form the oval base upon which the vase rested. In the Athenian vases the chins are normal in outline, and the necks of the two heads are moulded together so that the vase rested upon the flat circular base at the bottom of the neck. But the similarity of the two types is so pronounced as to leave no doubt in regard to their relation.

THE ETHIOPIAN TYPE ON PLASTIC VASES 31

From the ointment vase the type was soon adapted to pitchers and drinking cups with one or two handles. Some have single and some double heads.

The foregoing twenty-six vases showing Ethiopian heads have many characteristics in common. Practically all show the hair by means of tiny lumps of clay. In the technique introduced by the vase of Procles the skin is varnished black, while hair and lips are left in the color of the clay. The eyes are painted and sometimes additional details are added. All the vases show a desire for effective contrast. The hair was left dull in order to emphasize the shiny black skin. On the janiform vases the severe white face is introduced for sharp contrast. The white face and black cap are set over against the black face and dull hair. It is a type which recalls the archaic maidens from the acropolis. While the archaic smile is not pronounced, the large wide-open eyes recall the older technique.

The greatest contrast between the Greek and Ethiopian types was in features and skin. The regular, somewhat archaic nose and lips of the Greek girl offset the snub nose and protruding lips of the Ethiopian, and the pale color of her skin emphasizes the shiny, black flesh. One suspects from the spirited expression of these Ethiopian faces that the artist took the greatest pleasure in portraying them, and that the rather severe white face was introduced to contrast with the black, rather than the reverse.

The potter is more important than the painter in the case of these plastic vases. He created the mould into which these faces were pressed. That the Athenian plastic vases were pressed into moulds rather than poured can be seen from the fact that the insides of these vases are rough and show finger-marks. The points of the two parts are clearly visible on many examples. Often the lip was thrown separately on the wheel and attached. The rôle of the painter was secondary and consisted only of the painting of the features and head dress.

32 THE NEGRO IN GREEK AND ROMAN CIVILIZATION

Once the master potter had made the mould it could easily be used again either by the potter himself or by others in his workshop. In a number of instances we have replicas of plastic ware showing that this was done. "The Greek potter did not use the mould as a labor-saving device. He employed it only where the work demanded it, as in the Athenian plastic ware. Here we sometimes find the same mould used several times . . . but the number of such repetitions is not great, and certainly could not indicate mass production." [1]

A hunt for replicas among the Ethiopian heads shows the single heads all to be distinct and individual types. But on the double heads the same mould is employed seven times— on the Boston, London, and Paris ointment vases, the Bologna and Princeton drinking cups and the Brussels pitcher. On the Boston vase two Ethiopians are conjoined. On the others the Ethiopian is combined with a white girl. Likewise this Ethiopian is more masterly than the others. Who made this splendid mould, used in at least seven surviving examples?

Because the same mould of the white girl has been employed on another vase with the love-name Epilycus, these plastic vases have been attributed to Scythes, who employs the same name. On the face of it this seems slim evidence for assigning plastic vases to a man known only for painting. Perrot and Buschor come very close to the truth when they speak of these heads in conjunction with the beautiful head by Charinus in the Berlin Museum. No one seems, however, to have brought forward definite evidence connecting these double heads showing the negro type with Charinus, and the references have always avoided a definite assignment by references to the workshop or influence of Charinus or unknown artists of his circle. Even Buschor does not seem to know the signed fragments in the Villa Giulia Museum. [2]

To Charinus this finest of the negro heads can be assigned

---

[1] Richter, *The Craft of Athenian Pottery*, p. 28.
[2] Cf. *Not. d. Scavi*, 1916, pp. 53 ff.; Hoppin, *Handbook of Greek Black-figured Vases*, pp. 72-73.

THE ETHIOPIAN TYPE ON PLASTIC VASES   33

beyond possibility of doubt. The vase in Princeton and the
fragments in the Villa Giulia complete the evidence. The
white girl of the Princeton vase who is conjoined with the
Ethiopian head is identical with the single head in the Corneto
Museum which is signed by Charinus himself. The fragments of a negro head in the Villa Giulia Museum with a cup
mouth, similarly decorated showing it to be a companion piece
are also signed by Charinus. The fragments showing the ear,
hair and a bit of the skin are identical with the Ethiopian
mould used as the other half of the Princeton vase which we
know to be a replica of Charinus' signed vase. The other
vases are all replicas of this. It is not surprising that so
excellent a head as our negro should be the work of a man
whose skill as a potter is evident from the great beauty of his
signed vases.

But it is not necessary to suppose that Charinus always
used his own mould. In fact this is not possible for two of
the double heads are put together so badly that the adaptation
can not be the work of his own hand. The ointment vase
in the British Museum shows two heads put together entirely
without grace, and the Brussels pitcher leans and is not well
proportioned. The Boston, Paris, and Princeton vases are
well put together. It is likely that Charinus who made the
mould, modelled and signed the two vases in the form of
single heads with the cheese board pattern on the cup mouth,
and that the other vases were made by artists of his workshop
who had greater or lesser skill. This is further borne out by
the fact that the painted details differ greatly on the vases
from the same mould. On the signed Corneto vase the painting of the cap is very delicate and skilful, while on the Princeton vase it is very coarse.

Charinus made vases on which the painting was both black-
figured and red-figured. He is placed in the early fifth
century by Della Seta, but Buschor rightly places the girls'
heads by Charinus between the years 520 and 510 B. C. It
was known that Charinus made both pitchers and drinking

34 THE NEGRO IN GREEK AND ROMAN CIVILIZATION

cups. Now that the negro mould made by Charinus has been
identified with him, it is evident that he—or his workshop—
turned out ointment vases as well. As these are agreed to
have had an earlier popularity than the pitcher and drinking
cup styles, the dates 520-510 B. C. are not too early for
Charinus.

The single heads of Ethiopians, as we have said, so far
present no replicas. There is no chain of evidence connecting
any of them with known vase painters such as we have in
the case of Charinus. The majority belong in the transition
period between the two wares. The Boston cup with the
single handle has an elaborate black-figured design. The
Vienna cantharus is red-figured. Not many of the vases are
inscribed. No information is to be gained from the Vienna
cantharus. On the Athens vase the love-name Leagrus shows
the vase to be from the transition period as Leagrus' name
occurs on black-figured and red-figured ware alike. It can
not, however, help in identifying any one vase maker as it
occurs on vases, the work of at least fourteen men and many
others not yet identified. Calliades is known to be a maker of
plastic vases and some of the unidentified heads may some
time be brought into relation with him. Buschor believes the
Leagrus head to be the last of the series of Ethiopian heads in
Attic art.

The interpretation of these Ethiopian heads depends in
some measure on whether they are meant to represent men or
women. There is great disparity about this in the museum
catalogues. Even the Charinus mould is interpreted in both
ways. All doubt is removed here by the fact that the Brussels
pitcher shows the Ethiopian with a woman's cap of exactly
the same type as that of the white woman on vases. And no
one who is truly familiar with the negro type of our own
Southern cities can fail to realize that there is something
indefinably feminine about this head particularly when viewed
full in front. The oenochoe in Dr. Robinson's Collection and
the canthari in St. Louis and Vienna are clearly meant to be

THE ETHIOPIAN TYPE ON PLASTIC VASES   35

women, since the hair is bound up in a cap or turban similar
to that worn by the Ethiopian woman on the gem from the
Lewes Collection now in Boston. Negresses in Greek art are
not so rare as Dr. Seltman would have us believe when we
have at least eight instances before the fifth century is well
under way. On the other hand, the impression of certain
heads is as definitely masculine as these are feminine—for
instance, the Frankfurt and Boston cups with the single
handle.

The fact that the two sexes are shown on these vases pre-
cludes their interpretation as any one definite mythological
figure. Memnon and Andromeda were not considered black
in the sixth century before Christ. Dr. Seltman would like
to follow Mayor and see in the female Ethiopians a representation of the monster Lamia of Libyan origin, with whom Greek
mothers frightened their children. It is true that Dr. Robinson's vase shows large teeth which do not appear in the
others. In spite of this, however, the face does not seem sufficiently hideous for the conception of Lamia. She is more
probably a type which happened to interest the artist. The
other vases certainly are not meant to be Lamia. They are
not grotesques or caricatures—they are simply naturalistic.

Nor is there any basis for interpreting the off-set heads
from the point of view of any allegorical contrast such as day
and night. In such a case there would surely be some attri-
bute such as sun's rays or stars to call attention to the meaning. It is true that Pausanias in describing the Chest of
Cypselus relates that the woman who symbolizes Night holds
in her arms the two children Sleep and Death, the former
portrayed as white, the latter as black or dark (V, 18, 1),
probably in the same way as a woman holds two children on a
British Museum vase. However, the Greek word employed is
μέλας, which is nowhere a synonym for Αἰθίοψ. Death is elsewhere portrayed as black. If Death had been rendered with
the features of an Ethiopian, Pausanias would have specified
as he did in the case of the nude Ethiopian boy standing

36   THE NEGRO IN GREEK AND ROMAN CIVILIZATION

near Memnon in Polygnotus' painting of the lower world (X, 31, 7). It is improbable that the heads on these vases have any further significance than racial contrast for the sake of conviviality.

Helbig suggested that the Ethiopian on one of the double-heads was Busiris since it was coupled with Heracles. In the first place the Ethiopian probably represents a woman. Heracles is as well known as a heavy drinker as for his Busiris episode as witnesses Euripides' Alcestis; and in the second place there could be little point in combining Busiris with a white girl as on most of the vases, or Busiris with Busiris as on the Boston vase with the two Ethiopians. The same applies to the suggested identification of the white girl with Omphale, when she appears conjoined with Heracles. It would have no point when the white girl is conjoined with the satyr or Ethiopian. In the third place Heracles' drinking gives a hint as to the reason for the type. The vases in the form of heads have certain fixed types used singly or in combination—white girls, satyrs, Heracles, Ethiopians. Perrot suggests that the white girl is a nymph or Maenad. This is probably right, for although her features are in the severe and expressionless technique of the early period, she has a vine or garland on her head-dress. All but the Ethiopian type— nymphs, satyrs, the great drinker Heracles—are appropriate types for a revel or drinking bout. The Ethiopian—perhaps an echo of the Naucratis revellers—is a novelty, something to tickle the sense of humor and add to the gayety of the feast.

Granted that these Ethiopians are taken from life, as the Charinus negro certainly is, there is much left to guesswork as to what part they played in Athenian life in the sixth century. Probably they were first brought from Naucratis whither they had been brought from some region of the upper Nile. That they were slaves is without question. They were also indubitably a great novelty in sixth century Athens and would therefore be reserved for entertainment rather than for menial work. They waited on their master's tables at banquets, as

THE ETHIOPIAN TYPE ON PLASTIC VASES

their frequent presence on drinking cups would imply. As at least eight distinct types served as models there must have been at least eight, both men and women, in Athens. The others were probably sought as models after Charinus had popularized the type. There can be little doubt that he created a great demand for these Ethiopian vases when chance has preserved as many as eight replicas, a large number for a work-shop in Athens where vases were so seldom duplicated. The presence of Ethiopian boys on gems of the late sixth and early fifth centuries, together with these Ethiopian men and women is clear evidence of an established slave life for the race at Athens.

Everything, however, combines to show that they were never common in Athens and must have been rare in the sixth century. Theophrastus who wrote his *Characters* in the early third century has a man of " Petty Ambitions," who aims to do the fashionable thing at all times. This man is careful to have an Ethiopian for his attendant. Had Ethiopian slaves been common even in Theophrastus' time, it is not likely that the rich and fashionable would have affected them. They must have been unusual and expensive. From this it follows that they were even more rare at Athens two or three centuries before. One gets this feeling from the vases themselves, where the artist seems to have experimented in the portrayal of a new and curious race. There is no race prejudice even in the heads which offset the black type against the white. The contrast is shown in a spirit of sympathy which indicates that the artists saw in them comedy rather than homeliness.

A keen sense of the comic interest of the Ethiopians is the predominating element in the next use of the type on vases, a form which is the special study of Buschor in his article on Sotades. There exists a small group of vases, of Attic fifth century workmanship, in which a drinking cup mouth with red-figured painting is combined at the base with a plastic group showing an Ethiopian boy seized by a croco-

38   THE NEGRO IN GREEK AND ROMAN CIVILIZATION

dile. The two somewhat unrelated parts of the cup are
unified by making the tail of the crocodile curl up to form the
handle of the cup. The style of painting is different in each
case but the design of the plastic group is the same. The
crocodile has seized the Ethiopian's right arm in his jaws
and grasps him around the waist with his left forepaw, pulling him down on his right knee. The pose of the boy gives
the artist an opportunity to show his skill in modelling the
muscular structure, and there is striking realism in the pain
expressed by the wide open mouth and eyes. The conception
of the boy struggling in the grasp of the river animal inevita-
bly calls to mind the struggling Laocoon group, though the
latter is morbidly tragic and the former comic in intent. The
humorous effect is heightened by contrast with the gaiety of
the scenes painted on the cup mouth above. As Buschor
points out, the artist was familiar with the Ethiopian type
but not with the crocodile, since the animal is far from true
to life, particularly the head. He thinks it probable that the
artist conceived the idea of this plastic group from stories
of the Nile told by returned travellers. It seems more likely
that Sotades must have seen crocodiles at some time and have
attempted to reproduce them from memory. A vase signed
by him was found at Meroe and is now in Boston. If he had
never seen the animal it is improbable that the legs and claws
would be as well rendered. The Egyptian origin of the subject is now made certain by a faïence representation of a
crocodile with a severed negro's head by its side, recently
acquired by the Egyptian section of the Berlin Staatliche
Museum. It is published with illustrations in *Archäologischer
Anzeiger*, 1928, pp. 77-82. It resembles in style the faïence
ointment vases pictured by Buschor, *op. cit.*, figs. 49 and 50,
and is probably from the same factory, dating about 600 B. C.
An Italic rhytum in Naples (H. 2958) with a severed negro's
head, shows the continuance of the type (*Arch. Anz.*, 1928,
p. 81, figs. 3 and 4).

The theory which Buschor sets forward in his article is

FIGURE 9.

CROCODILE AND NEGRO.   FIFTH CENTURY B. C.

In Munich.

THE ETHIOPIAN TYPE ON PLASTIC VASES   39

that this group of vases, together with others in the form of
animal heads, can be assigned to Sotades, from the resemblance between the bands of painting on the cup mouths and
the painting on other vases which are signed works of Sotades.
The article was worked out in such detail as to leave little
room for doubt, but it has been confirmed beyond dispute by
the finding of Sotades' signature upon the vase from Meroe in
the form of a rhytum with a cup mouth, now in the Boston
Museum of Fine Arts.[3] The plastic group at the base is a
horse and rider. Buschor is interested mainly in the animal
and the band of painting; but he has also assembled many
instances of the Ethiopian type in connection with the figure
on these vases, and has made a classification of the vases in
the form of plastic heads which paved the way for Sotades'
crocodile group. As has been said, he failed to complete the
identification with Charinus.

These Attic fifth century vases are the earliest examples
of the comic association of negro and crocodile, a motif very
common in the magazines of humor a generation ago and still
found in the souvenir statuettes sold at southern resorts.
Buschor distinguishes between the crocodile vases which are
of genuine Attic fifth century workmanship, and those of
later Italian workmanship which were made to imitate them.
The Attic examples are the following:

57. Boston—Museum of Fine Arts, 98, 881. Cf. *Annual Report*,
1898, p. 72, no. 48; *Arch. Anz.*, 1899, p. 145, 48; Buschor,
Mün. Jb. Bild. Kunst, XI, 1919, p. 3, no. 3, pls. 1 and 2, figs.
32 and 33.

Drinking cup, the lower part a plastic group of an Ethiopian boy struggling with a crocodile. The cup mouth is
ornamented by a band of red-figured painting showing two
satyrs and two Maenads. The crocodile was painted green,
with details added in black. The Ethiopian's flesh was
painted black. Eye-lids, eye-brows and hair were painted

---

[3] Cf. *Boston Museum Bulletin*, April 1923; Hoppin, *Handbook of
Greek Black-figured Vases*, p. 474.

40   THE NEGRO IN GREEK AND ROMAN CIVILIZATION

brown, the lips red and the teeth white.   Ht. 0.24 m., length
of base 0.202 m.

58. Van Branteghem Coll.—formerly Tyskiewisz Coll. Cf. *J. H. S.*,
IX, 1888, p. 220, fig. 2; *Hoffman Sale Cat.* no. 99; Froehner,
Coll. Branteghem, 291, pl. 48; Buschor, *Mün. Jb. Bild. Kunst*,
XI, 1919, p. 3, no. 4, and p. 4, fig. 3.

Vase similar to the foregoing. The band of painting on
the cup mouth is different, but has the same subject, i. e.,
satyrs and Maenads. Ht. 0.255 m.

59. Dresden—Albertinum—from Nola. Cf. Buschor, *Mün. Jb. Bild.
Kunst*, XI, 1919, p. 3, no. 2, figs. 2 and 34.

Vase similar to the foregoing. The band of painting is
poorly preserved, but the four figures on it were warriors and
women. Ht. 0.225 m.

60. Munich—Museum Antiker Kleinkunst—from Italy. Cf. Buschor,
Mün. Jb. Bild. Kunst, IV, 1912, p. 74; Buschor, *Mün. Jb.
Bild. Kunst*, XI, 1919, p. 2, no. 1, figs. 1 and 35; Sieveking,
Arch. Ans., XXVIII, 1913, p. 22, fig. 2, no. 12.

Vase similar to the foregoing, but much restored. The
band of painting shows two maidens, one in hunting garb and
two draped figures. Ht. 0.235 m. Fig. 9.

To these vases which are genuine Attic examples, Buschor
adds another which probably belongs in this class:

61. Catania—Museo Biscari. Cf. F. de Roberto, *Catania* (Bergame,
1907) p. 122; Buschor, *Mün. Jb. Bild. Kunst*, XI, 1919, p. 4,
no. 5.

Vase similar to the foregoing. It is decorated only with a
lozenge pattern and branches, which are arranged over each
other in the manner of a frieze.

It is evident that there was slight use of the Ethiopian as
a subject for archaic terra-cottas. One specimen is listed
from Athens and the museum catalogue calls it a negro. No
illustration is available by which to judge the racial type,
though the catalogue calls the work crude. Since only one
example seems to occur it is possible that the figurine is not
intended for an Ethiopian, the crudity of the work having
made this a plausible supposition.

THE ETHIOPIAN TYPE ON PLASTIC VASES 41

62. London—British Museum—from Athens. Cf. Walters, *Terracottas*, p. 75, B 27.

Archaic terra-cotta figurine of an Ethiopian (?) on horseback with a basket of fruit in front of him. The back of the figure is not modelled.

There are only a few gems of the fifth century which represent the negro. An agate scarab, dating from the first quarter of the fifth century, of excellent Etruscan workmanship from Corneto, now in Boston, shows a little negro attendant holding a sponge and squatting on the ground in front of Peleus (Beazley, *The Lewes House Collection of Ancient Gems,* pl. A, 16). A Greek intaglio of the free style of the end of the fifth century, now also in Boston, shows the head of a negress with an ample kerchief wound about it. The frizzled hair appears in front and behind. She wears earrings and a necklace. It is a wonderful head with warm, rich modelling, a real masterpiece (Beazley, *op. cit.,* pl. 3, 52). The negro appears also for a brief period on the coinage of Athens and Delphi (cf. Seltman, *Athens, Its History and Coinage,* pp. 97, 200).

CHAPTER IV

THE FIFTH CENTURY—THE ETHIOPIAN TYPE IN VASE PAINTINGS.

In leaving the plastic vases and passing over to the Ethiopian type in vase painting, the mythology surrounding Ethiopia is again encountered. The myths of Greece and their representation in contemporary drama were a favorite subject of the vase painter. When the Attic artist undertook to reproduce a scene which involved characters connected with this legendary country, it was natural that he should give them the features of the Ethiopians whom he had seen, and who had already been established as an appropriate subject by the moulders of plastic vases. None of the actual rulers of Ethiopia who appear as principals in these vase paintings are themselves portrayed as black, just as they are not black in the literature. It is only such attendants, soldiers and slaves as are introduced into the scene who are given the genuine Ethiopian physiognomy. The artists could not give the ruling caste the features which they associated with a group of slaves of their own time.

There are four legends which involved the Ethiopians in their representations on Greek vases. The stories of Memnon and Andromeda, concern chiefly the mythical Ethiopia of the east; the Busiris legend is related to Egypt; and the story of Lamia is connected with Libya.

Memnon, hero of the *Aithiopis* and of Attic tragedy, appears on many vases, the principal subjects being his victory over Antilochus, his fight with Achilles watched by the two goddess mothers, Eos and Thetis, and the grief of Eos at his death. In proportion to the many vases showing Memnon in battle, very few show Ethiopian attendants. None of the vases showing the mourning for Memnon show followers of the Ethiopian type. As in Greek literature, when the Dawn Goddess is the important figure the idea of dark Ethiopians

42

THE ETHIOPIAN TYPE IN VASE PAINTINGS 43

is submerged. But when armed Ethiopians appear on vases they undoubtedly are connected with the Memnon myth, even when the principal character Memnon is absent. Only those vases showing Ethiopians will be given here. For the others see G. E. Lung, *Memnon: Archäologische Studien zur Aithiopis.*

The vases which portray Memnon with his Ethiopian warriors all show the same scene, Memnon standing between two Ethiopian warriors.

63. London—British Museum. Cf. Gerhard, *Auserles. Vasenb.*, III, pl. 207 and p. 117; Panofka, *Arch. Zeit.*, 1846, pl. 39, figs. 2 and 3; Loeschke, *Arch. Zeit.*, 1881, p. 31, n. 9; Loeschke, *Bonner Studien*, p. 248; Schneider, *Jb. Kunst. Samml.*, III, 1885, p. 4, n. 5; *Wiener Vorlegebl.*, 1889, pl. III, 3 b and 3 c; Karo, *J. H. S.*, XI, 1899, p. 140; Walters, *Catalogue of Vases*, II, p. 138, B 209; Buschor, *Mün. Jb. Bild. Kunst*, XI, 1919, p. 36; Robinson, *A. J. A.* 1908, p. 433; Hoppin, *Handbook of Greek Black-figured Vases*, p. 110.

This black-figured amphora in the style of Execias shows Memnon armed for battle and attended on either side by an Ethiopian. These two attendants are given with great realism. Their hair is woolly, their foreheads sloping and wrinkled, their noses snub and broad. One wears a short chiton and carries a pelta, the other wears a cuirass and short chiton. Both carry clubs in their right hands.

There is an inscription, Amasis, and some obscure letters which were at first read as ἐποίησεν but the name refers to the fallen negro. See Philadelphia vase below.

64. Munich—Sammlung König Ludwigs. Cf. Schneider, *Jb. Kunst. Samml.*, III, 1885, p. 4, n. 6; Jahn, *Beschreibung der Vasensamml.*, no. 541; Buschor, *Mün. Jb. Bild. Kunst*, XI, 1919, p. 37.

This amphora shows Memnon and his Ethiopian attendants, the latter characterized by great prominence of jaw. It is of later date and poorer workmanship than the London amphora.

65. New York — Metropolitan Museum. Cf. Furtwängler, *Sitzb. Mün. Akad.*, 1905, pp. 274-5; Buschor, *Mün. Jb. Bild. Kunst*, XI, 1919, p. 37.

This black-figured amphora, similar to the Execias amphora

44   THE NEGRO IN GREEK AND ROMAN CIVILIZATION

in London, shows an armed hero standing between two Ethiopians.

The vases on which Memnon does not appear, but which can undoubtedly be connected with the *Aithiopis* are the following:

66. Berlin—Coll. of Dr. Brueckner. Cf. *Arch. Anz.*, XXVIII, 1913, p. 35.

Two fragments of a red-figured lutrophorus very finely drawn. Instead of a wedding scene there is a battle with portions of two Ethiopians. Dr. Brueckner assigns them to the Memnon episode.

67. Erlangen—Universitaetssamml. Cf. Buschor, *Mün. Jb. Bild. Kunst*, XI, 1919, p. 38, pl. 3.

Three fragments of a large red-figured amphora. On one a bearded and helmeted Greek warrior is piercing an Ethiopian with his spear. The piece is broken so that the Ethiopian's eyes and the top of his head are gone, and his figure is broken off at the waist, but the woolly hair and prominent jaw reveal the race of the figure. The other two fragments show the face and body of a second Ethiopian who is lying upon the ground. The closed eyes show him to be dead. The features of the Ethiopians are somewhat idealized, and there is no trace of the comic or grotesque in their pain such as is present in the crocodile vases.

68. Naples—National Museum—from Cumae. Cf. Heydemann, *Die Vasensammlung des Museo Nazionale*, p. 864, no. 172; Schneider, *Jb. Kunst. Samml.*, III, 1885, p. 4, n. 6; *Gaz. Arch.*, XXIX, 1904, p. 208; Graindor, *Musée Belge*, XII, 1908, p. 31; *Mon. Ant.*, XXII, 1913, pl. LXI; Buschor, *Mün. Jb. Bild. Kunst*, XI, 1919, p. 38.

On this polychrome lecythus an Ethiopian warrior with a slight beard is arraying himself in heavy armor. He wears helmet, cuirass and chiton, and a chlamys hangs behind him. His sword is hanging from his lance, which is in front of him, and he is raising his shield from the ground with both hands. Buschor suggests that the man is Memnon himself arming for battle. This is unlikely, as the vase is too early for Mem-

THE ETHIOPIAN TYPE IN VASE PAINTINGS   45

non himself to be thought of as Ethiopian. It is probably one of his followers.

69. Paris—Louvre—from Sommavilla. Cf. Welcker, *Bullettino*, 1837, p. 73; Schneider, *Jb. Kunst. Samml.*, III, 1885, p. 4, n. 6; Pottier, *Vases Antiques du Louvre*, II, 1901, p. 153, G 93, pl. 99.

Archaic red-figured cylix, whose interior design is an armed Ethiopian, running. He is nude, but a chlamys placed over his right shoulder hangs down on either side of his body. He holds a lance in his right hand, and carries on his left arm a shield in the shape of a pelta, decorated with a vine of black ivy. His lips are thick, his nose short and his jaw structure very prominent. In the field are some letters of an inscription, but they have not been interpreted.

Pottier says that the provenance of the vase is unknown, but it tallies in every detail, even to the illegible inscription, with the vase described by Welcker in the *Bullettino*, for 1837, p. 73. Diam. 0.33 m.

70. Philadelphia — University of Pennsylvania Museum — from Orvieto. Cf. Bates, *Transactions, Dept. of Arch., Univ. of Pa.*, I, 1904, pp. 45-50, Pls. I and II; Furtwängler, *Sitzb. Muen. Akad.*, 1905, pp. 257-258, 20; D. M. Robinson, *A. J. A.*, XII, 1908, p. 433; Lung, *Memnon*, pp. 28-31; E. H. Hall, *Museum Journal*, VI, 1915, pp. 91-2, fig. 68; Buschor, *Mün. Jb. Bild. K.*, XI, 1919, p. 37; Hoppin, *Handbook of Greek Black-figured Vases*, p. 111.

This black-figured amphora has scenes from the Trojan war, probably as related in the *Aithiopis*. On one side an armed warrior, probably Ajax, is bending over the body of Achilles, while Menelaus is killing an Ethiopian who is inscribed AMAꟄOꟄ and who is rendered realistically with the blood spurting from his wound. On the reverse the corpse of Antilochus lies on the ground, and three armed Greek warriors are pursuing two nude figures meant to be Ethiopians, though the faces of these have gone. Amas(i)os is probably the genitive of Amasis, as Achilles' name is also given in the genitive. He bears a marked resemblance in features and equipment to the Ethiopian marked Amasis on the London amphora. Both carry the crescent-shaped shield and the club.

46   THE NEGRO IN GREEK AND ROMAN CIVILIZATION

Only the pose is different. Amasis on the London vase appears with Memnon; on the Philadelphia vase he has just received a severe, probably fatal wound. The name Amasis was at first wrongly taken to be the signature of the painter in both instances. Loeschke rightly assigned the London vase to Execias, while D. M. Robinson and Furtwängler assigned the Philadelphia vase to the same master. That the vases are the work of one hand is evident from the close resemblance of the two negroes.

The most labored interpretation of the word Amasis was probably that of Leaf, who thought it referred to the white corselet of linen like those sent by King Amasis of Egypt, thus showing the Egyptian origin of Memnon. This idea became untenable when the recurrence of the word Amasis on the Philadelphia vase became known. Beyond question the name refers to the Ethiopian, even though he is not otherwise known. The natural conjecture (since these vases are too early for the Greek dramas in which Memnon figured) is that he is a character from the *Aithiopis,* some trusty Ethiopian follower of Memnon. The Ethiopian with a crescent-shaped shield on the red-figured cylix in Paris is probably this same Amasis. Perhaps this shape of shield was mentioned in the *Aithiopis* as the epic poets often gave descriptions of armor (as for example the shield of Heracles). If this Amasis is indeed an Ethiopian character of the *Aithiopis* the vases tell us at least this much of his rôle: that he was a companion of the armed Memnon and supported him in his duel with Antilochus. After the death of Antilochus he was pursued off the field by Greek warriors. He survived his master and after the death of Achilles finally met death at the hands of Menelaus.

Buschor connects also with the Ethiopian warriors of Memnon the trumpet blowers who appear as a shield device on several vases. Chase includes these Ethiopian trumpeters under the class of devices chosen to indicate rank, such as armed human figures and horsemen. This seems possible,

THE ETHIOPIAN TYPE IN VASE PAINTINGS   47

since it was undoubtedly a sign of distinction to have a rare
negro slave at the time when these vases were painted. On
another vase not mentioned in Chase's article the shield device
is two Ethiopians with a serpent between them. The function
òf the negroes may be apotropaic as well. This would not
preclude the other explanations. The Ethiopian appears as a
shield device on the following vases:

71. London—Rogers Coll. Cf. Welcker, *Annali*, 1845, pp. 154-155;
     Alte Denkmaeler, V, p. 388, no. 24; Schneider, *Jb. Kunstb.
     Samm.*, III, 1885, p. 4, n. 6.

On this hydria, whose principal design is the judgment of
Paris, are two warriors who hold one shield between them.
The shield device is a serpent between two Ethiopians, one of
whom is armed with a bow and quiver, the other with a club.
Welcker adds " Ce sont, sans doute, des soldats de Memnon."

72. Vienna—K. K. Oest. Museum—Castellani Coll., 4626. Cf. Mas-
     ner, *Samml. Antiker Vasen*, p. 49, no. 332, pl. VI; Chase,
     Harvard Studies, XIII, p. 114, CLXXXI; Buschor, *Mün. Jb.
     Bild. K.*, XI, 1919, p. 38, n. 12.

An Ethiopian occurs as a shield decoration on this Attic
red-figured amphora. He blows a long trumpet which he
holds in his right hand. A mantle hangs over his right
shoulder and left arm. His left arm and knees are bent in
a comic attitude.

73. Würzburg—formerly Feoli Coll. From Vulci. Ht. 0.575 m. Cf.
     Urlichs, *Verzeichniss der Antikensamml.*, III, 302; *Mon. Ant.*,
     I, pl. XXXV; Welcker, *Alte Denkmaeler*, III, pl. XXVI;
     Mueller-Wieseler, *Denkmaeler der Alten Kunst*, I, 44, 209;
     Overbeck, *Galerie Heroischer Bildwerke*, pl. XV, 4; Bau-
     meister, *Denkmaeler*, I, p. 725, pl. XIII, 779; F. R. II, pp.
     226-229, pl. 104; Chase, *Harvard Studies*, XIII. p. 114,
     CLXXXI; Buschor, *Mün. Jb. Bild. Kunst*, XI, 1919, p. 38,
     n. 12; Reinach, *Répertoire des Vases*, I, 77.

An Ethiopian with a long war trumpet occurs as a shield
device on this black-figured amphora. He is nude except for
a band at his waist from which are suspended a sword and
sheath. The features are of pronounced Ethiopian type, and
the angle of the left arm with hand resting on the left hip
gives a comic effect. A piece is broken out so that the lower
part of the figure is missing. Baumeister suggests that the

48 THE NEGRO IN GREEK AND ROMAN CIVILIZATION

shield device may have a proleptic reference to the defeat of Memnon by Achilles, on whose shield it appears. Reinach says that the vase is attributed to Amasis, but neither Karo nor Hoppin accept it as an unsigned vase of Amasis.

With Memnon's followers have been associated a much discussed group of *alabastra,* all of which have practically the same design very crudely painted in black on a dull white ground. In all, the principal figure is an Ethiopian wearing a sleeved jacket and trousers. He walks toward the spectator's right, but his head is turned in the opposite direction. The arms are extended awkwardly at right angles to his body. In his right hand he usually holds a double axe, and over his left arm is spread a folded piece of cloth. On the majority of these vases there is in the background a palm tree and an altar or table. On a few examples a Corinthian or Boeotian helmet is lying either on the table or on the ground. The vases follow:

74. Athens — National Museum — from Thebes. Cf. Heydemann, *Arch. Ztg.,* XXX, p. 36; Reinach, *Rev. Arch.,* 1913, I, 99; Winnefeld, *Ath. Mitt.,* XIV, 1889, p. 42; Cecil Smith, in Petrie, *Naucratis,* I, p. 51; Corey, *De Amaz. Ant.,* p. 89; Collignon-Couve, *Catalogue des Vases,* p. 338, no. 1088 (—2082); Graindor, *Musée Belge,* XII, 1908, p. 25, no. 8.

75. Athens—National Museum—from Thebes. Cf. Reinach, *Rev. Arch.,* 1913, I, p. 99; Corey, *De Amaz. Ant.,* p. 89; Winnefeld, *Ath. Mitt.,* XIV, 1889, p. 42; Collignon-Couve, *Catalogue des Vases,* p. 338, no. 1089; Graindor, *Musée Belge,* XII, 1908, p. 25, no. 7.

76. Athens—National Museum—from Athens. Cf. Reinach, *Rev. Arch.,* 1913, I, p. 99; Corey, *De Amaz. Ant.,* p. 89; Winnefeld, *l. c.,* p. 43; Collignon-Couve, *Catalogue,* p. 339, no. 1090 (—2960); Graindor, *l. c.,* p. 25, no. 9.

77. Athens—National Museum—from Tanagra. Cf. Winnefeld, *l. c.,* p. 43; Reinach, *Rev. Arch.,* 1913, I, p. 99; Collignon-Couve, *Catalogue,* p. 339, no. 1091 (—3515); Graindor, *l. c.,* p. 25, no. 10.

78. Athens—Sale—from Laurium. Cf. Graindor, *l. c.,* p. 26, no. 15.

79. Athens — found at Athens — fragment found in pre-Persian débris. Cf. Bethe, *Ath. Mitt.,* XV, 1890, pp. 243-245; Graindor, p. 26, no. 16.

80. Berlin—Antiquarium—from Naples c. 1833. Ht. 0.145. Restored from fragments. Cf. Heydemann, *Arch. Ztg.,* 1872,

THE ETHIOPIAN TYPE IN VASE PAINTINGS 49

p. 27; Furtwängler, *Beschreibung der Vasensamml.*, II, p. 532, no. 2260; Winnefeld, *l. c.*, p. 42, n. 2 and p. 44; Bethe, *l. c.*, p. 243; Reinach, *Répertoire des Vases*, I, p. 412, no. 6; Graindor, *l. c.*, p. 25, no. 6; Corey, *De Amaz. Ant.*, p. 90.

81. Boston—Museum of Fine Arts. Cf. *Arch. Anz.*, XIV, 1899, p. 144, no. 36; Buschor, *l. c.*, p. 37, n. 11.

Vase like the foregoing.

82. Boston—Museum of Fine Arts. Cf. *Arch. Anz.*, XIV, 1899, p. 144, no. 37; Buschor, *l. c.*, p. 37.

Vase in the form of a girl's head, with a vase mouth upon which this same Ethiopian figure appears.

83. Brussels—private coll. Cf. Graindor, p. 26, no. 17.

84. Brussels—*Musée du Cinquantenaire*. A 1391—from Laurium. Cf. Graindor, *l. c.*, figs. 1 and 2.

85. Compiegne. Cf. Heydemann, *l. c.*, p. 37, A; Graindor, *l. c.*, p. 25, no. 3.

86. Copenhagen—from Athens. Cf. Ussing, *Nye Erhvervelser til Antiksamlingen i Kjöbenhavn*, N. 6; Bethe, *l. c.*, p. 245, n. 1.

87. Dresden. Cf. *Arch. Anz.*, 1889, p. 170—from Crete (?); Buschor, *l. c.*, p. 37, n. 11.

88. Durand Coll. Cf. Buschor, *l. c.*, p. 37, n. 11; Schneider, *Jb. Kunst. Samml.*, III, 1885, p. 4, n. 6.

89. Gerona—from Ampurias. Cf. Frickenhaus, *Emporion*, nos. 123 and 126; Reinach, *Rev. Arch.*, 1913, I. p. 99; Buschor, p. 37, n. 11.

One has an individual in Persian or Eastern garb chasing an Ethiopian.

90. Kertch—Novikow Coll. Cf. *Arch. Anz.*, XII, 1897, p. 7.

91. London—British Museum—from Tanagra. Cf. Corey, *De Amaz. Antiq.*, p. 89; C. Smith, *Naucratis*, I, p. 51; *Catalogue of Vases in the British Museum*, II, p. 297, B 674; Graindor, *l. c.*, p. 25, no. 1.

92. Naples—Branteghem Coll. Cf. Heydemann, *l. c.*, 1869, p. 36, no. 10 and no. 115; Heydemann, *l. c.*, 1872, p. 35; Froehner, *Coll. Branteghem*, p. 64, no. 155; Froehner, *Deux Peintures de Vases Grecs*, p. 17; Reinach, *Répertoire des Vases*, I, p. 412, no. 5; Graindor, *l. c.*, p. 25, no. 4; Reinach, *Rev. Arch.*, 1913, I, p. 99.

This Ethiopian has bow and arrow instead of ax.

93. Parent Coll.—from Camirus. Cf. Froehner, *Deux Peintures de Vases Grecs*, p. 17; Heydemann, *Arch. Zeit.*, 1872, p. 35 C; Winnefeld, *l. c.*, p. 41; Bethe, *l. c.*, p. 244; Corey, *l. c.*, p. 90; Graindor, *l. c.*, p. 25, no. 1.

50 THE NEGRO IN GREEK AND ROMAN CIVILIZATION

Corey suggests that this is the same as the Naucratis vase, but the origin is apparently not the same.

94. Paris—Louvre. Cf. Graindor, *l. c.*, p. 25, no. 5; Froehner, *Deux Peintures*, p. 17.

95. Paris—Louvre.

There is a second vase of this type in the Louvre. Cf. Corey, p. 90.

96. Paris—Druot Sale. Cf. *Vente Druot,* 1904, no. 147, pl. IX; Buschor, *l. c.*, p. 37, n. 11.

97. Paris — Lambros Sale. Cf. *Vente Lambros*, 1913, no. 39; Buschor, *l. c.*, p. 37, n. 11.

98. ?—from Rhodes. Cf. C. Smith, *Naukratis*, I, p. 51; Graindor, *l. c.*, p. 26, nos. 13 and 14.

99. Tarentum — found at Tarentum. Cf. Bethe, *l. c.*, p. 243; Graindor, *l. c.*, p. 26, no. 18.

Round plate with figures of the same style as on the alabastra and with the inscription.

100. Tübingen — University Coll. — Inv. 1362. Watzinger, *Griech. Vasen*, p. 40, no. 51, fig. 20; no. 47, pl. 16.

Fragment of the inside of a plate showing a young negro boy wearing a jacket with sleeves. He has the same pose as those on the alabastra. The work is finer. His nose, lips, and jaw are well shown. His hair is indicated by an outline of curly dots.

101. Athens—Private Coll.—from Megara. Cf. Winnefeld, *l. c.*, p. 44, fig. p. 45; Graindor, *l. c.*, p. 25, no. 11.

The history of the discussion about these vases is as follows: Froehner first called attention to this type of alabastrum. He assembled four examples of the type, and this number has been increased in subsequent articles by other authorities so that now at least twenty-eight examples have been published. In the following year the alabastra were discussed by Heydemann, and Cecil Smith assigned the series to Naucratis from the technique and the subject as well as from the fact that three of the examples were excavated at Rhodes, where the influence of Naucratis was strong. He agreed with Froehner in considering that the figures repre-

THE ETHIOPIAN TYPE IN VASE PAINTINGS 51

sent Ethiopian Amazons, since several such vases exist where
the figure has a white face. On such vases, however, the palm
tree, ax, table, and cloth are similar.

Winnefeld considered that the vases probably contained
some product coming from Egypt, and that the recurring
Ethiopian type was a sort of advertisement or announcement
of the contents. Gardner's opinion that they came from
Naucratis was overthrown when a fragment of a plate of the
same fabric and with the same subject, but with an Athenian
inscription, was published by Bethe. Bethe's interpretation
was that they are a proof of the active commercial relations
between Egypt and Athens at the beginning of the fifth century. Corey does not believe the figures to be Amazons, white
or Ethiopian, nor does he see in them a reference to the
Memnon story. He agrees with Winnefeld that the type was
chosen as a sort of trade advertisement.

A new list of eighteen such vases was formed by Graindor.
His view is that these Ethiopians are Asiatic, since their costume is the one generally given on vases to Amazons, Scythians and in general all barbarians who come from Asia. This
is strengthened by the fact that on one example are two
Ethiopians wearing Phrygian caps. Graindor believes that
the figures are all soldiers, armed with the double axe and
using the folded cloth as a shield. He argues that Herodotus
lists Ethiopians among the armies of Xerxes and that they
had probably fought at Marathon; and that it is no serious
objection to his views that Herodotus describes a different
costume from the one which appears on the vases. Since the
Ethiopians were defeated together with the Persians,
Graindor believes that this series of vases was made to flat-
ter Greek vanity. He sees in the helmet a dedicated trophy
which is a delicate reference to the Greek victory, and
believes that the Ethiopian is supposed to be in flight.

Reinach, while agreeing that the vases were beyond doubt
made at Athens and show some relation between that city
and the Greek colonies in Egypt, is inclined to agree with

52 THE NEGRO IN GREEK AND ROMAN CIVILIZATION

Froehner in thinking them Amazons such as appeared in combat in the opening of the Aithiopis. Perrot agrees with Winnefeld and sees in them merely a trade advertisement. They were made quickly and exported by the hundreds, hence the crudity of the drawing. Their type was a novelty and therefore became suddenly and widely popular. Buschor considers that a reference to the Memnon myth is intended. Pfuhl sees only the commercial advertisement of a favorite Egyptian perfume. D. M. Robinson suggests a connection between the Ethiopians, who as we know from gems served as bath slaves, and these alabastra containing unguents used at the bath. In this case the Ethiopian type would symbolize the bath.

The only agreement of opinion seems to be that the vases were of Athenian manufacture, were widely exported and symbolized some relationship with Egypt. The interpretations of the Ethiopian figure differ widely. That they were made at Athens is proved by the fact that two of them have Athenian inscriptions and that one such figure occurs on the popular type of vase in the form of a head. That they were widely exported is proved by their varying provenance, two having been found even in Spain. The relationship with Egypt is evident from the type of alabastrum which was used in both countries and possibly from the Ethiopian figure as well.

The view that the figure was an advertisement is undoubtedly correct. For this reason it was repeated over and over again. But merely because it degenerated into a repeated trade-mark when it became popular, it does not follow that it was originally a trade-mark only. The device when adopted must have had some particular meaning or must have made some reference to a place or event intelligible to the Greeks. Otherwise why all the details of dress—the palm tree, the table or altar and the helmet? Graindor's view that the alabastra symbolize the Greek victory over the Ethiopians who came in Xerxes' army is untenable. It is true that the

THE ETHIOPIAN TYPE IN VASE PAINTINGS   53

costumes suggest Asia; but the other points made by Graindor are open to serious objection. In the first place the representation of a contemporary event is unusual in Greek art, particularly in contrast with Roman which is so predominantly commemorative. Aeschylus did bring the Persian war upon the Greek stage, but in a tragedy of dignified proportions, mentioning no Greek by name and placing the scene at distant Susa. Likewise it seems inconsistent with the Athenian pride in their tremendous victory to commemorate it in art by picturing a humble and almost grotesque auxiliary. Another argument against the interpretation is that at least four of the vases have been found at sites in Boeotia, and such a design would not be popular in a state which Medized. Furthermore, if the helmet is to be regarded as a dedicated trophy, why is it a Greek helmet? Would not some trophy more of an African or Asiatic nature have been selected? The principal argument is that fragments of one vase were found in Persian débris on the Acropolis, thus dating their manufacture before the Persian wars.

There are not such serious objections to the Memnon interpretation. In this case the Greek helmet would be that of the fallen Greek warrior Antilochus who had just been slain by Memnon. The helmet has been dedicated at the altar as a trophy and one of Memnon's warriors looks back at it as he leaves the scene. The Asiatic dress is appropriate since they are assisting the besieged city of Troy in Asia. Likewise according to one version of the story Memnon came to Troy by way of Persia, with which he was closely associated in legend. On the other hand, it is impossible to be certain that an Ethiopian Amazon is not meant, fresh from a successful duel with a Greek warrior. To those who knew the *Aithiopis* the whole scene was probably clear.

It is not likely that the interpretation will be settled to the satisfaction of everyone. The use of an Asiatic scene to symbolize an African perfume does not sound consistent on the surface. However one must not expect any consistency in

5

54   THE NEGRO IN GREEK AND ROMAN CIVILIZATION

regard to Ethiopia. As has been shown in connection with
the literature, the Greek mind was in complete confusion as
to Ethiopia and considered it now in the East, now in Africa.
A scene from the *Aithiopis* would be accepted without question as symbolic of Africa at this time when genuine Ethiopians who were so rare in Athens· and interest in whom was
so great, were known to have come from Africa.

Compared with the Memnon legend, other myths yield
comparatively small returns in the way of representations of
Ethiopians in art. A few occur on vases connected with the
story of Andromeda, daughter of Cepheus and Cassiopeia.
Her mother boasted rashly about her beauty, saying that she
was fairer than the Nereids, and thus incurring the dis-
pleasure of Poseidon, who sent a sea monster against the
land. The oracle said that the only way of escape was to
deliver up Andromeda to it, and Cepheus in order to save his
people had his daughter bound to a spot where she would be a
prey to it. Perseus, returning from his victory over Medusa,
slew the sea monster, freed the maiden and married her,
though she had previously been betrothed to a certain
Phineus. Just as Memnon himself is never represented with
negro features, neither are these rulers of Ethiopia, though in
later times the Roman Ovid describes Andromeda as swarthy.
In literary tradition Andromeda went down as black, e. g.,
in the Andromède of Corneille.

One vase shows Phrygians, not Ethiopians, as the servants
of Cepheus, but genuine Ethiopian faces occur on certain
vases, which are listed below:

102. Berlin—Antiquarium 3237—Formerly in Branteghem Coll.—
     From Capua. Cf. Bethe, *Jb. Arch.* XI, 1896, pp. 292-300, pl.
     II; Furtwängler, *Arch. Anz.*, VIII, 1893, pp. 91-92, fig. 50.

This crater illustrates the Andromeda story. The principal
characters in the scene are Andromeda, Perseus, Cepheus,
Aphrodite and Hermes. There is in addition a seated figure
wearing a long-sleeved jacket and gayly ornamented trousers.
There is a wreath on the hair and the features are unmistak-
ably Ethiopian. This figure has been the subject of contro-

THE ETHIOPIAN TYPE IN VASE PAINTINGS 55

versy. It was interpreted by Froehner as a woman personifying Ethiopia. Furtwängler considers it neither a woman nor an allegorical reference to Ethiopia but offers no solution of its meaning. Bethe agrees with Furtwängler that the figure is masculine, from the clothing and the absence of any indication of the breast. He says that the figure can not be a servant since he does not carry any paraphernalia. He believes that the vase portrays Euripides' version of the Andromeda story; that the costumes are undoubtedly those of the stage and that the Ethiopian is a female figure. While this is an ingenious interpretation, it is not all impossible that the Ethiopian is a woman and that she represents Ethiopia. Personification of cities and countries was not infrequent in classical art. The figure on the Andromeda vase in London wears the same type of costume. In the fifth century Athenian fancy had confused the Ethiopians and the Amazons. The figure is obviously not meant for a servant or she would not be seated in the presence of the rulers. She is evidently of equal importance with them and the allegorical interpretation seems satisfactory. It would show that the scene of the story was Ethiopia. The vase was made in Attica about the end of the fifth century.

103. London — British Museum — Canino Coll.—from Vulci. Cf. *Archaeologia*, XXXVI, pp. 53-70, pl. VI; *Annali*, 1872, pp. 108-130; Robert, *Arch. Ztg.*, 1878, p. 16; Tümpel, *Jb. Phil. Paed.*, Suppl. XVI, p. 129 ff; Bosanquet, *J. H. S.*, XIX, 1899, p. 177; Petersen, *J. H. S.*, XXIV, 1904, pp. 99-112, pl. V; F. R., pl. 77, text II, pp. 94-97; Walters, *Catalogue of Vases*, III, pp. 152-153, E 169.

This hydria shows the chaining of Andromeda, not to a rock according to the more usual version of the myth, but to two upright posts. The scene is being watched by Perseus, at the extreme right, and next to him is Cepheus wearing a tiara and seated on a throne. At the center of the picture is a figure wearing a sleeved jacket and trousers, and a tiara, and supported by two Ethiopian slaves, each holding up an arm of the supported figure. To the right of this group are three Ethiopians who are preparing the ground and the stakes,

56   THE NEGRO IN GREEK AND ROMAN CIVILIZATION

and to the left of the group are three more who are bringing up objects for the funeral rites. The supported figure is the subject of dispute. Petersen wishes to interpret it as Phineus, the betrothed suitor of Andromeda, from the height of the figure and the masculine dress, and thinks that he is bringing up the funeral objects for the sacrifice of his betrothed. The chief objection to this interpretation is that if the figure is to be taken as Phineus, the main character, Andromeda herself, is not shown on the scene. Also, this figure has the most important position in the scene, the center, and the arms are in the proper position to be fastened to the upright stakes which are already being fixed in the ground. Likewise the piteous expression is more appropiate to the victim than a mourner only. She is taller than the slaves who hold her up, but her importance in the story warrants this. Both sides of the scene converge toward this figure which is the center of interest, and it seems unlikely that it could be anyone but the heroine herself. If this depicts the Andromeda of Sophocles, and the tradition was that the Andromeda was a satyric play, there is nothing wrong in making the central figure somewhat comic or of a height greater than the others. The eight Ethiopians have thick woolly hair, short noses and thick lips, and one has a wrinkled forehead which shows, according to Walters, that he is older than the others.

The myth of Busiris in vase painting began with the remarkable Caeretan hydria. It is probable that this adventure of Heracles almost immolated on the altar of Busiris and suddenly breaking free, the persecutors becoming victims, had been popularized early by Sicilian and Attic comedy. This vase showed both Egyptian priests and Ethiopians, whereas the majority of the Attic representations of the story show only Egyptians. The usual type for such priests assisting at the sacrifice is the low forehead, shaved head and long mustaches. On certain of the vases, however, the type is plainly Ethiopian or the Egyptians have been given a negroid appearance. There

THE ETHIOPIAN TYPE IN VASE PAINTINGS 57

are a number of vases on which the story is shown, but only the following show the Ethiopian type:

104. Athens—Central Museum. Cf. Dumont-Chaplain, *Céramiques de la Grèce propre*, pl. XVIII, text pp. 379-381; Hartwig, *Meisterschalen*, p. 55, n. 1; Herzog, *Studien zur Geschichte der griechischen Kunst*, pl. VI, 2.

This red-figured amphora of the severe style, shows the scene of Heracles at the altar attacking the priests of Busiris. He wears the lion skin and holds one of the priests or servants in the air by the feet. To the right of the altar, another servant holds a double axe with both hands above his head as if about to strike (cf. the double axe held by the Ethiopians on the series of alabastra). A third figure who has crouched down on the ground has his arms raised in an attitude of fear. Pottier remarks that the type has frankly turned toward the grotesque, and that the bald crania and burlesque attitudes suggest satyric drama actors. This is probably the correct interpretation since it is known that Euripides wrote a satyr play around the Busiris story and that it was a favorite with the comedy writers. It is probable that the different priests who appear on the vases go back to different comedies or satyr plays as originals.

105. Berlin—Antiquarium—Canino Coll.—from Vulci. Cf. Stephani, *Compte Rendu*, 1868, p. 41; Gerhard, *Trinkschalen u. Gefaesse*, pl. VIII, p. 9; Dumont-Chaplain, I, p. 580, no. 9; Furt-wängler, *Vasensamml.*, II, p. 714, 2534.

On this red-figured cylix, the scene on the exterior shows Heracles being led to the sacrifice, bound, by two barbarians of Ethiopian type. A third walks in front of him, carrying a lecythus.

106. Bologna—Museo Civico. Cf. Zannoni, *Scavi della Certosa*, pl. 23, no. 10; Schneider, *Jb. Kunst. Samml.*, III, 1885, p. 6, n. 8; Heydemann, *Hall. Winckelmannspro.* VII, p. 62, no. 117; Dumont-Chaplain, I, p. 380, n. 7; Pellegrini, *Necr. Fels.* p. 60, no. 174.

Amphora with a scene from the Busiris story. Two Ethiopians with stump noses hold sacrificial instruments. One is bearded. The hair of both is rendered by raised and varnished dots.

58 THE NEGRO IN GREEK AND ROMAN CIVILIZATION

107. Munich—König Ludwig's Coll.—from Vulci. Cf. *Bullettino*, 1829, p. 109, no. 28; Helbig, *Annali*, 1865, p. 300; Dumont-Chaplain, I, p. 580, no. 8; Jahn, *Vasensamml. König Ludwigs*, p. 107, no. 342.

Hydria with the Busiris story. The Ethiopians are of a type similar to those on the Athens and Bologna vases, and wear ear-rings.

108. Oxford — Ashmolean Museum — Oldfield Coll. Cf. Helbig, *Annali*, 1865, p. 300, pl. PQ; Gardner, *J. H. S.*, XXIV, 1904, pp. 306-7.

Stamnus with the scene from the Busiris story which shows Heracles turning on his tormentor and the negroes in confusion. The attendants are Ethiopian with woolly hair shown in dots in the same manner as on plastic vases and gems. The vase was known to Helbig from a drawing only. It has since come into the possession of the Ashmolean Museum.

109. Naples—National Museum—from the Basilicata. Cf. Gerhard, *Neapels Antik. Bildw.*, 375, n. 30; Millingen, *Peint. de Vases*, 28; Helbig, *Annali*, 1865, p. 302, IV; *Musée Borb.* XII, 38; Heydemann, *Vasensamml.*, p. 333, no. 5258; Dumont-Chaplain, I, p. 380, no. 12.

Fragment of a large red-figured crater with the Busiris story. Busiris himself wears a Phrygian cap. The attendants are two maidens and two barbarian slaves of Ethiopian type. Nude Ethiopians hold Heracles chained between them. One is crouching on the ground.

110. Athens—for sale. Cf. Buschor, *Mün. Jb. Bild. Kunst*, XI, 1919, p. 40, fig. 55.

Fragment of a red-figured vase showing the upper part of an Ethiopian who is carrying in his hand two sacrificial spits and therefore is probably to be associated with the Busiris legend. He is markedly dolichocephalic and the outline of his woolly hair is indicated by a wavy incised line. His nose is short and his lips are everted, making the racial type very pronounced.

The foregoing myths have had Asiatic or Egyptian associations, but the myth which Mayer wishes to see represented on a vase in Athens is connected with Libya.

THE ETHIOPIAN TYPE IN VASE PAINTINGS 59

111. Athens—National Museum. Cf. Mayer, *Ath. Mitth.*, XVI, 1891, pp. 300-312, pl. IX; Seltman, *A. J. A.*, XXIV, 1920, p. 15; Collignon-Couve 961; Buschor, *Ath. Mitth.*, LII, 1927, pp. 230 ff.

This white Athenian lecythus, dating about 480 B. C., with decoration in black, shows a woman of grotesque and horrible aspect tied to a palm tree and tortured by five satyrs. Mayer wishes to recognize in this figure Lamia, a witch-like creature who was the bogey of Greek children. She had been a Libyan queen beloved by Zeus, and the jealous Hera had deprived her of her children. In her frenzy Lamia stole the children of other people, and from the cruelties which she practised on them became a hideous and distorted person. The vase seems to fit the myth, for the woman's figure is most horribly distorted. Likewise Zeus gave her the power of taking out her eyes and putting them back, so that when they were out she was quiet but when they were in she went on her frightful raids. The woman on the vase seems distinctly to have empty eye sockets, which probably accounts for her helplessness at the hands of the satyrs.

This striking scene of cruelty is so strange a conception for Greek art that Mayer is undoubtedly right in associating it with some dramatic presentation, particularly from the presence of the satyrs. Buschor, however, thinks it unlikely that Lamia should be represented as a negress and that satyrs should be punishing the vampire. He connects the scene with some satyr-drama based on the story in Pausanias I, 23, in which perhaps satyrs appeared as apes, and violated the woman put ashore on the apes' islands. This interpretation seems to be an improvement over Mayer, who suggests the travesties on myths which are known to have been performed at the Cabiric sanctuary at Thebes and which are reflected in the vases found there. This interpretation would connect the vase with another group of Cabiric vases upon some of which one of the famous characters of Greek mythology is frankly caricatured as an Ethiopian. Lamia had African ancestry, and it is not surprising to find her portrayed as a negress.

60 THE NEGRO IN GREEK AND ROMAN CIVILIZATION

But there is no such tradition in the case of the enchantress Circe, and to find her rendered with Ethiopian features is an instance of the intentionally grotesque.

The Circe vases of this type are as follows:

112. Baltimore—Coll. of Prof. D. M. Robinson. Cf. *A. J. A.*, XIX, 1915, p. 79 and XXI, 1917, p. 87.

This is an unpublished scyphus with black painting on a dull buff ground. A triple band of brown paint runs around the center of the vase, and a wider single band at the top. Between these are the designs; on one side a grapevine, on the other a scene in caricature of Circe offering Odysseus a potion. Odysseus on the right is on his knees and receives the bowl with both hands. His hair is portrayed in comic disorder, and his features are grotesque. Circe, at the left, stands with her back to her loom, dressed in a loose garment and holding the bowl out to Odysseus. Her features are caricatured but not strongly Ethiopian as on the Oxford and London vases described below.

113. Cambridge, Mass.—Coll. of Prof. Hoppin, Fogg Art Museum. Cf. *A. J. A.*, XIX, 1915, p. 79; *Corpus Vasorum Antiquorum*, *U. S. A.*, I, pl. 5.

A Cabiric vase which caricatures the Circe myth, but on which Circe is probably not Ethiopian.

114. London—British Museum. Cf. Walters, *J. H. S.*, XIII, 1893, pp. 77-87, pl. IV.

This scyphus from the Cabirium is similar to the foregoing. It has on one side the grapevine pattern like that on Dr. Robinson's vase, and on the other the scene of Circe offering Odysseus the potion in a scyphus-shape vase. Circe is frankly caricatured as a negress. Her nose is short and snub, her lips thick and her jaw protruding. Her hair is fastened in a turban-like cap. She wears a loose garment and her pose is purposely ungraceful. She stands at the left of the scene facing Odysseus, and is identified by the inscription above her head. Odysseus is shown as an emaciated figure, nude except for a cloak thrown about his shoulders and a pointed cap. He

THE ETHIOPIAN TYPE IN VASE PAINTINGS 61

wears a sheathed sword and leans on a knotted staff. His legs are crossed and his attitude comic. Back of him is Circe's loom, and at the extreme right one of his companions who has been transformed into a bear.

115. Oxford—Ashmolean Museum—formerly Branteghem Coll. Cf. Froehner, *Sale Catalogue*, Branteghem Coll., no. 210; Walters, *J. H. S.*, XLII, 1893, p. 79 and fig. 2, p. 80; Gardner, *Greek Vases in the Ashmol. Mus.*, p. 19, no. 262, pl. 26.

On this scyphus from the Cabirium the same episode is shown in caricature. Odysseus is at the left of the picture and is shown in full front, whereas the other vases show him in profile. He wears the travelling hat and his cloak hangs over his arm. His body is grotesquely distorted. At his right, in profile, stands Circe facing him, stirring a potion in a scyphus. She wears a long flowing garment. As on the London vase, she is evidently meant to be an Ethiopian, from her nose, mouth and jaw. It is difficult to determine whether the black dots on her head are intended to represent curly hair or the pattern of a cap. Back of her is her loom and shuttle. The care with which all the slender threads of the loom are represented is proof that the apparent crudity of the figures is intentional.

These vases date from the late fifth or early fourth centuries. One other instance of caricature, from an earlier period than the Boeotian vases, shows the probable intention of the artist to give Ethiopian features to one of the figures he represents:

116. Paris—Louvre—from the Cyrenaica. Cf. Perrot, *Le Triomphe d'Hercule*, 1876, pl. 3; Schneider, *Jb. Kunst. Samml.*, III, 1885, p. 6, n. 8.

The vase is the famous caricature of the triumph of Heracles, driven in a chariot drawn by centaurs, by a Victory who is of a distinctly non-Greek type. Perrot (p. 22) says that she has the snub nose, thick lips and square jaw of a negress, and that since the vase was intended for Africa, the artist wished to give one of his principal personages the traits which belong to the physical type of entirely African popula-

62   THE NEGRO IN GREEK AND ROMAN CIVILIZATION

tions.   Perrot has exaggerated the negroid characteristics of
the victory, though she does undoubtedly suggest the African
type.

This closes the list of vases which can be definitely associated with any of the myths of Greece.   There still remain a
few vase paintings where Ethiopians are represented in some
of the slave functions which they performed in everyday life.
They make no pretence to direct caricature or the grotesque,
though it is impossible to dissociate from the comic any realistic representation of a genuine Ethiopian.   These occur-
rences of the type are unrelated having in common only the
fact that they are all genre scenes:

**117. Athens—Acropolis.   Cf. Buschor, *Mün. Jb. Bild. K.*, XI, 1919,
p. 40 and p. 41, fig. 56.**

This fragment of a red-figured vase shows the upper part
of an Ethiopian boy.   He is evidently the slave of the person
whose hand is seen at the left of the fragment and who is
engaged in pouring ointment from a vase.   The scene is
similar to one on a gem in the Corneto Museum, where an
Ethiopian slave boy is crouching down on the ground near
his master, who is also pouring ointment from a vase.

**118. Berlin—Antiquarium—from Eretria.   Cf. Bosanquet, *J. H. S.*,
XIX, 1899, p. 173, pl. III; Fairbanks, *Athenian Lecythoi with
Outline Drawing in Glaze Varnish*, pp. 259-260, no. 5; Riezler,
Weissgrundige Attische Lekythen, pl. 25, text, p. 104; Buschor,
Mün. Jb. Bild. Kunst, XI, 1919, p. 40.**

An Athenian lecythus with a grave scene.   At the right of
the stele is a Greek woman holding a lecythus in her hand.
To the left of the stele, facing her, is a slave girl carrying a
stool on her head and an alabastrum in the right hand.   Her
nose is snub, her lips thick and her hair short and wavy.   She
is certainly a barbarian and the profile verges toward the
Ethiopian type.   Bosanquet says she " is not necessarily a
negress," but it seems probable that she is so intended when
one compares her with the Ethiopian stool-bearer on the
Andromeda hydria in the British Museum.   Bosanquet also

THE ETHIOPIAN TYPE IN VASE PAINTINGS   63

notes a similar profile on a small lecythus at Cambridge (Gardner, *Catalogue of the Fitzwilliam Mus.*, p. 59, no. 138, pl. XXX) but the type of this figure is simply barbarian, not Ethiopian.

119. Copenhagen. Cf. Ussing, *To Graeske Vaser*, Copenhagen, 1866, p. 7, pl. I; Bosanquet, *J. H. S.*, XIX, 1899, p. 177; Beazley, *Attic Red-figured Vases*, p. 63; Buschor, *Mün. Jb. Bild. K.*, XI, 1919, p. 40.

Red-figured amphora, on one side of which is shown an old man out walking, attended by an Ethiopian slave boy.

120. ? —Hope Collection. Cf. Tillyard, *The Hope Vases*, No. 121, pl. 19.

Kalyx-Krater H. .30 m. Broken and mended, the surface rubbed. B. three draped youths. A. Two actors and two satyrs. One actor a bald, beardless negro slave holding a torch. He wears an animal skin and carries a torch. The other actor is dressed like a king and holds a scepter. One satyr is lighting his torch from that of the slave, who is unconscious of what is going on. Undoubtedly the negro is a comic figure in some satyr play.

120. Waterklyn Sale Cat. 97 B. Cf. Tischbein, III, pl. 19; Müller-Wieseler, II, 6, pl. 48, no. 603; Reinach, *Rep. d. Vases*, II, 314; Tillyrand, *The Hope Vases*, p. 71, no. 121, pl. 19.

121. Munich—König Ludwigs Coll. Cf. Jahn, *Beschreibung der Vasensamml.*, p. 88, no. 301; *Arch. Zeit.*, 1854, pl. LXVI; 1866, pl. XCV; Reinach, *Rep. des Vases*, I, p. 396.

One of the followers of Theseus on a red-figured vase is a boy with thick lips and curly (though not woolly) hair. He is dressed for travelling, and wears hat, chiton, chlamys and boots. Over his left shoulder is a skin which serves as a travelling sack. In his right hand he holds a club. The outfit is unusual for Ethiopians and one may not be meant here.

122. Paris—Louvre—Campana Coll. Cf. Pottier, *Vases Antiques*, 2 serie, p. 154, G 100, pl. 99; Pottier, *Catalogue des Antiques*, part III, 1906, p. 926.

Fragment of a red-figured cylix, the interior scene depicting a nude Ethiopian carrying an oenochoe. He is evidently the

64   THE NEGRO IN GREEK AND ROMAN CIVILIZATION

slave of the man whose shoes appear at the right of the fragment. The Ethiopian's nose is short and broad and his thick lips hang open.

123. Leningrad—Hermitage—Campana Coll. Cf. Stephani, *Compte Rendu*, 1875, pl. V; Schneider, *Jb. Kunst. Samml.*, III, 1885, p. 7, n. 4; Reinach, *Répertoire des Vases Peints*, I, p. 49; Buschor, *Mün. Jb. Bild. Kunst*, XI, 1919, p. 40.

One of the figures on this pelike is an Ethiopian bald-headed boy who leads a camel by the halter. Behind the camel is a palm tree. A similar figure is found on a silver patera of Assyrian origin now in the Louvre, where one of the figures in a procession is an Ethiopian leading a dromedary.

124. Vienna—Cf. Bosanquet, *J. H. S.*, XIX, 1899, p. 177.

This polychrome lecythus shows a youth who is going toward Charon's boat, attended by an Ethiopian slave who carries a bird cage and a hare. The slave wears a turban and his face is painted black.

125. ?—Cf. *Monumenti*, VIII, 1856, pl. IX; Schneider, *Jb. Kunst. Samml.*, p. 7, n. 2.

One of the figures in this vase painting of late style is a nude Ethiopian boy, who carries two stools.

These vases invite some comment both as to their success in portraying the Ethiopian type and what they show of the usual function of the Ethiopian slaves at the time they were made. Bates [1] has made the statement that "as a rule, the negro is most absurdly drawn on Greek vases." This comment was inspired by the Caeretan hydria, though it seems strange that in spite of certain archaic limitations of the vase Bates should fail to respond to the vigor and spirit there shown. "Most absurdly drawn" is a dubious phrase. It is hard to say whether Dr. Bates means "most comically" or "most badly." Neither is true, however, "as a rule." On

---

[1] Cf. *Transactions, Department of Archaeology, Univ. of Pennsylvania*, I, 1904, p. 50.

THE ETHIOPIAN TYPE IN VASE PAINTINGS   65

certain vases, as has been seen, the effect is intentionally comic and on a few others the drawing is such that one can not readily tell whether the artist intended the figure to be an Ethiopian or a barbarian. It must be borne in mind, however, that the painter of red-figured vases had several handicaps to overcome. The technique itself prevented him from giving the figure a black skin and thereby making his intention instantly clear. Nor was it as easy to indicate woolly hair as in the case of the plastic vases with their raised dots. As has been seen the vase painter in several instances borrowed this technique and reproduced the woolly hair by dots. Unable to show the dark skin and not always certain of how to portray that non-Greek woolly hair the painter was deprived of the two most prominent Ethiopian characteristics. Neither was there any characteristic and easily recognizable Ethiopian dress. He, therefore, fell back upon the short nose, thick lips, or prominent jaw as being the principal features by which to depict the negro physiognomy. For this reason it is reasonably sure that when any two of the above features occur the vase painter is attempting to portray an Ethiopian. That they varied greatly in skill is to be as much expected as that they would vary in portraying the white race. The Ethiopians of Execias surpass the one drawn by the painter of the Ethiop Pelike.

The vases show that the Ethiopian slaves are still reserved for personal attendance. They are not menial laborers. All the vases with genre scenes show them as personal servants or followers. They are associated with the bath by the vase on which an Ethiopian is pouring ointment and another on which he carries an oenochoe. A young mistress on a lecythus is attended by a slave carrying a bird cage. An Ethiopian boy attends an old man, a maid servant carries a stool and alabastrum for her mistress. An Ethiopian boy carries two stools for visitors. The Ethiopian leading a camel is probably a reminiscence of an Egyptian trip made by some artist. The occupations are not heavy labor. The only suggestion of hard

66 THE NEGRO IN GREEK AND ROMAN CIVILIZATION

work occurs on the Andromeda vase where Ethiopians are driving stakes in the ground, and this is unquestionably a scene from a play.

While Ethiopians were still rare at this time, they were kept as attendants doubtless because their masters found them diverting and amusing. They were likewise considered comic as their presence on the stage proves. Their chief popularity as a stage figure was evidently in comedies and satyr plays. In nearly all the vase paintings referring to mythology their rôle was a comic one. The Athenian seeing them daily at the palaestra and frequently upon the comic stage began to take them for granted. They no longer held the same mystery at the close of the fifth century as when they first appeared upon the streets of Athens.

CHAPTER V

THE ETHIOPIAN TYPE IN THE FOURTH CENTURY

During the fourth century the popularity of the Ethiopian race as an art subject seems to have waned at Athens. Doubtless the novelty of their appearance had worn off considerably, and the tendencies in art which made them a furore in the Hellenistic period which followed, had not as yet developed. This century was the period of their great popularity in Magna Graecia. The Greeks of southern Italy had imported some of the Attic vases in the form of Ethiopians heads, and had taken a particular fancy to the crocodile drinking cup of Sotades. Realizing the possibilities of a vogue for these, local vase makers evidently decided to imitate rather than import, and in consequence we have a series of these vases, of obvious fourth-century Italian workmanship.

There is no difficulty in differentiating the imitations from the Attic fifth-century originals. The Italian artists altered somewhat the proportions of the vase; they added ornamental details to the decoration of the crocodile, and twisted his tail about the Ethiopian's left arm. Hence it no longer served as a handle for the cup, and another handle was added above it. The simple painting, usually of four human figures, which Sotades put upon the cup mouth, gave way to the more florid painting of the period, which ran down over the whole of the cup mouth instead of being restricted to a band.

A few have even altered the posture of the Ethiopian, so that his right leg instead of his right arm is held in the crocodile's mouth, and he is lashed to the body of the cup by the crocodile's tail. Another example, while keeping the traditional posture of the figure, has replaced the cup by a trefoil pitcher mouth. These imitations or adaptations are of interest for the painting of the crocodile, since the paint is gone from the animals on the Attic vases. The modeling

67

68   THE NEGRO IN GREEK AND ROMAN CIVILIZATION

of the crocodile is no more true to life than in the originals and shows no closer acquaintance with the reptile. Although the Ethiopians must have been known to the south Italian Greeks by a period as late as the fourth century, these stiff little black figures with staring eyes have no individuality and have evidently been copied from the Attic vases, not from life. There is no advance in the rendering of the racial type. The technique has been taken over, though with little skill, and if the Italian vases show a more striking contrast between black skin and white eye-balls, it is because the paint on most of them has been better preserved.

An interesting variation of the crocodile drinking cup is in the Jatta Collection. The band painting on the cup mouth, especially the figure of the winged victory, is so similar to that of a crocodile vase in the same collection that the two must be the work of the same hand. But while the shape of the cup, the band of painting and even the design on the pedestal are similar, the body of a maiden with a dog in front of her, has been affixed to the crocodile's tail forming a representation of the sea monster Scylla. The fish tail given to Scylla is longer than that of the crocodile, but retains the gaudy stripes and spots given the crocodile on all these Italian vases which were copied from the Attic originals where the plastic dots remain although the paint has disappeared. Cf. J. E. Harrison, *Myths of the Odyssey,* p. 195, pl. 55 b; Buschor, *Mün. Jb. Bild. Kunst,* XI, 1919, p. 6, no. 10.

The Apulian vases of the type of the Ethiopian boy seized by a crocodile are as follows:

126. Cambridge—Fitzwilliam Museum—Earl of Cadogan Coll. Cf. Gardner, *Catal. of Fitzw. Mus.,* p. 80, no. 244, pl. XXXVI; Buschor, *l. c.,* p. 6, no. 8, fig. 8;

127. London—British Museum—from Capua. Cf. Walters, *Catal. of Vases,* IV, p. 191, F 417; Buschor, *l. c.,* p. 5, no. 7.

128. Naples—National Museum—Santangelo Coll.—from Ruvo. Cf. Panofka, *Arch. Anz.,* 1849, p. 60, 3; Heydemann, *Vasensamml.* p. 648, no. 42; Buschor, *l. c.,* p. 6, no. 13.

129. Naples—National Museum—Santangelo Coll.—from Ruvo. Cf. Heydemann, *Vasensamml.,* p. 648, no. 44; Buschor, *l. c.,* p. 6, no. 14.

THE ETHIOPIAN TYPE IN THE FOURTH CENTURY   69

130. Paris—Bibliothèque Nationale—Coll. Janzé 157. Cf. A. de Ridder, *Catalogue des Vases*, II, p. 673, no. 1252, pl. XXXIII; Buschor, *l. c.*, p. 6, no. 11.

The vase has a trefoil pitcher mouth instead of the usual cup mouth.

131. Paris—Louvre—Campana 3836. Cf. Buschor, *l. c.*, p. 6, no. 12. The vase has a trefoil pitcher mouth. *Ruvo—Jatta Coll.*, 1268. Cf. Buschor, *l. c.*, p. 6, no. 10, fig. 8.

The following vases differ in the shape of the cup mouth but the grouping of Ethiopian and crocodile is identical. The crocodile holds in his jaw the right foot of the Ethiopian and pins down the Ethiopian's left foot with his claw, while he lashes the neck of the Ethiopian with his tail.

132. Berlin Antiquarium—Sabouroff Coll.—from Ruvo. Cf. Furt-wängler, *Beschreibung der Vasensamml.*, II, p. 944, no. 3408, Buschor, *l. c.*, p. 7, fig. 10.

133. Leningrad—Hermitage 367—from Apulia. Cf. Reinach, *Antiquités du Bosphore Cimmerien*, 2nd ed., p. 87, Buschor, *l. c.*, p. 7.

134. Ruvo—Jatta Collection—1460. Cf. Buschor, *l. c.*, pp. 7-8, fig. 11.

Still another variant is that found on a vase in Berlin where the crocodile has seized the arms and waist of a boy (not clearly marked as Ethiopian because of indistinguishable features but undoubtedly intended for one because of the association of negro and crocodile), as on the Attic vases. The feet of the boy are not separated as on all the other vases but are brought together as if the boy were being dragged or lifted.

135. Berlin Antiquarium—from Capua. Cf. Furtwängler, *Beschreibung der Vasensammlung*, II, p. 991, no. 3893; Buschor, *l. c.*, p. 8, fig. 12.

The great similarity between all these vases, even those whose design has been altered, points to one place of manufacture, and the fact that so many have been found at or near Ruvo points to a workshop here. The local demand must have been the stimulus to manufacture, as practically none of these vases were found outside of Italy.

70   THE NEGRO IN GREEK AND ROMAN CIVILIZATION

The negro and crocodile do not again appear in classical
art as a plastic group although the subject of the following
Italian vase painting must be related to the foregoing group
as it was done about the same time and comes from the same
place.

136. Naples—National Museum—Mus. Borbonico—from Ruvo.   Cf.
Heydemann, *Vasensamml.*, p. 449, no. 2958; Buschor, *Mün.
Jb. Bild. K.*, XI, 1919, p. 43.

This is a drinking cup with a band of painting depicting
a boy running away from a crocodile, at which he is looking
back.   Below the animal is a small Ethiopian's head in relief.
Italian work.   Ht. 0.22 m.

The vase in the form of the Ethiopian's head evidently
enjoyed the same kind of popularity and underwent the same
kind of imitation on the Italian peninsula as the crocodile
group.   Furtwängler has said of the imitations that they
" lack the characteristic strength of the Attic Moors' heads."
Not only is the expression of the face rendered with less
masterly skill, but just as the painting of the negro-crocodile
vases became more florid the simplicity of effect has been
weakened by the addition of wreaths, ribbons and other
painted details which bridge the way to the developments of
the Hellenistic period which followed.   There is some advance
in that the little raised dots of clay which had heretofore been
used to suggest the curls have been replaced in some instances
by an attempt at actual modelling of the hair, and there is
more use of incised lines in adding details.   There are no
more janiform vases, all that occur being examples of the
single head type:

137. Berlin—Antiquarium—San Canino Coll.—from Vulci.   Cf.
Panofka, *Delphi u. Melaine, Berlin Winckelmanns Program*,
IX, p. 6, nos. 3 and 4; Furtwängler, *Beschreibung der Vasen-
samml.*, II, p. 831, no. 2870.

This drinking cup has a single handle and large mouth, in
the form of an Ethiopian's head.   Panofka rightly considers
that it is meant to represent a woman, from the head-dress of
ribbon bands, painted red, which cross each other over the

THE ETHIOPIAN TYPE IN THE FOURTH CENTURY   71

forehead and either ear. The curly hair is indicated by raised spirals like snail shells. The eyes are deep-set, the cheeks hollow, the nose short and broad and the lips protruding. There is no life in the expression of the face. Ht. 0.202 m.

138. Berlin—Antiquarium—Sabouroff Coll.—from southern Italy. Cf. Furtwängler, *Beschreibung der Vasensamml.*, II, p. 945, no. 3411.

Vase with narrow pitcher mouth, in the form of an Ethiopian's head. The flesh is painted black on a white slip. The hair is in rows of curls, and the lips are red. Above the head is a thick yellow cushion band with ends hanging down on the shoulder. Ht. 0.12 m.

139. Berlin—Antiquarium—Sabouroff Coll.—from southern Italy. Cf. Furtwängler, *Beschreibung der Vasensamml.*, II, p. 945, no. 3412.

Vase with a narrow pitcher mouth, in the form of an Ethiopian's head. Furtwängler suggests that a woman is meant, since the hair is decorated with a wreath. The flesh is painted black on a white slip. Ht. 0.123 m.

140. Berlin—Antiquarium—Sabouroff Coll. Cf. Furtwängler, *Beschreibung der Vasensamml.*, II, p. 969, no. 3665.

Vase from Italy with an Ethiopian's head in relief on the handle.

141. London—British Museum—Castellani Coll.—from Capua. Cf. Walters, *Catalogue of Vases*, IV, p. 263, G 156.

Ascus in the form of an Ethiopian's head, interesting for its use of coloring. A wreath around the front of the head, with flowers at each end, is painted white; eyes and teeth are painted white; and red is used for the eye-brows and lips. Ht. 2¼ in.

142. London—British Museum. Cf. Walters, *Catalogue of Vases*, IV, p. 262, G 155.

Oenochoe in the form of the head of an Ethiopian, with thick curly hair. The forehead is wrinkled, and over it is a heavy garland which falls in a loop over each ear. This vase was found on the island of Cos, but Walters assigns it to

72   THE NEGRO IN GREEK AND ROMAN CIVILIZATION

fourth-century workmanship, and it is therefore contemporary
with the Italian vases. Ht. 4¼ in.

**143a. Baltimore. Found by D. M. Robinson in 1928 at Olynthus.
Vase of red clay, in form of negro head, 0.15 m. high, 0.12 m.
wide, 0.09 m. thick.**

Large coarse outstanding ears with deep opening. Wide
flat nose with spreading nostrils. Thick lips and receding
chin. Protruding eyes. Pronounced supra-orbital ridges.
Receding forehead with one deep wrinkle. Hair in coarse
curls extending down to ears and out over forehead in large
mass. Top of vase and neck and bottom broken. Before
348 B. C. Fig. 10.

**143b. Saloniki. Vase in form of negro head found by D. M. Robinson
in 1928 at Olynthus. From broken top to base of neck, 0.155 m.
Widest part of head by ears, 0.105 m. Face alone, 0.065 m.
wide. Thickness, 0.09 m. at eyes, 0.103 m. at mouth. Diameter
of top opening, 0.039 m., of base, 0.075 m. Before 348 B. C.**

Hair acts like wreath around the head and anticipates such
Hellenistic vases as Figures 16 and 17. Figs. 11 and 12.

**144. Paris—Bibliothèque Nationale. Cf. De Witte, *Cabinet Durand*,
no. 96; Panofka, *Delphi u. Melaine, Winckelmannsprogram*,
IX, p. 7.**

One-handled drinking cup in the form of the head of an
Ethiopian woman. She wears a *sphendone* set with stars and
a laurel wreath. Panofka suggests that the stars may be
intended to mean that she represents night. Ht. 0.15 m.

The other objects belonging to the fourth century have
nothing in common beyond their period and the evidence that
the popularity of the type survived in widely different areas.
No one interpretation will cover them all.

There are a few asci from Cyprus where the Ethiopian type
had been so popular in the sixth century and was probably at
that time considered apotropaic. This may still have been
the feeling in the fourth century, as the small heads moulded
on the top of the asci are in full front. A similar ascus from
Greece in the Stoddard Collection, however, looks more as if
the asci belong purely in the realm of genre without ulterior

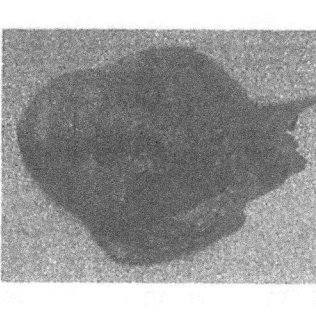

FIGURE 10.
VASE IN FORM OF NEGRO HEAD FROM OLYNTHUS.
Presented to Johns Hopkins University by the Greek Government.

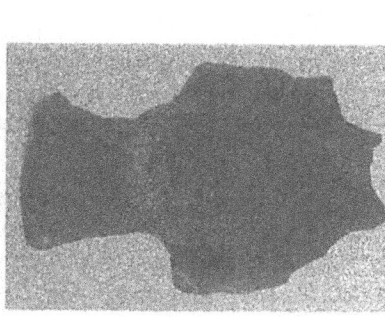

FIGURE 11.
VASE IN FORM OF NEGRO'S HEAD FROM OLYNTHUS.

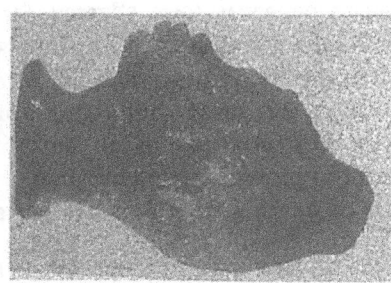

FIGURE 12.
SIDE VIEW OF FIGURE 11.

THE ETHIOPIAN TYPE IN THE FOURTH CENTURY   73

intent. This is not the case with a group of engraved gems from Sardinia. There is marked oriental influence to be seen in these gems, some of which show the Ethiopian head strongly conjoined with other heads not negroid. The prophylactic theory is the most reasonable explanation of these, since the types seem to be of intentional ugliness.

To this century belongs also, Wace notwithstanding, the fine bronze head of an African in the British Museum, a portrait, doubtless idealized, which has been the subject of much discussion summarized below, but which is too isolated a case to affect the general development of the Ethiopian type in Greek art. Aside from this bronze and the Sardinian gems, the use of the Ethiopian type in the fourth century is confined to vases; and these are chiefly imitations of an earlier period at the same time that they hint of Hellenistic developments to come.

The objects follow:

Asci

145. Cambridge—Fitzwilliam Museum—from Cyprus. Cf. Myres-Richter, *Catalogue of Cyprus Museum*, p. 88, no. 1772.
Ascus with an Ethiopian's head in front view moulded in relief upon the top.

146. Cyprus Museum. Cf. Myres-Richter, *Catalogue*, p. 88, no. 1772.
Ascus similar to the foregoing.

147. New Haven—Stoddard Collection, Yale University—from Greece. Cf. Baur, *Catalogue of the Stoddard Coll.*, p. 209, no. 357.
Ascus with a trumpet-shaped spout and arched handle. In a large convex medallion on the top is the mask of an Ethiopian in full front. He has woolly hair and wears ear-rings in the shape of fleur-de-lys. Superior Greek fabric of the fourth century.

148. Paris—Louvre, Room H, no. 333—from Cyprus. Cf. Myres-Richter, *Catalogue of the Cyprus Museum*, p. 88, no. 1772.
Ascus similar to the Cambridge and Cyprus Museum examples.

74 THE NEGRO IN GREEK AND ROMAN CIVILIZATION

GEMS

149. Cagliari Museum—from the necropolis at Tharros, Sardinia. Cf. Furtwängler, *Antike Gemmen*, I, pl. XV, no. 83; II, p. 73, no. 83.

Scarab of green jasper with the head of an Ethiopian in profile to right. The gem is not well preserved and the outlines of the face are somewhat blurred, but the broad nose and thick lips show the race of the subject. The scarab is of Phoenician style.

150. London—British Museum—from Tharros. Cf. Smith, *Engraved Gems*, p. 51, no. 161, pl. C.

Green jasper scarab with the bust of an Ethiopian in profile to right. The woolly hair is indicated· by raised dots close together. The lips are thick and the cheek-bones prominent.

151. London—British Museum—from Tharros. Cf. Smith, *Engraved Gems*, p. 52, no. 179, pl. C.

Green jasper scarab showing two conjoined heads, a bearded male head in full front and an Ethiopian in profile. The nose of the Ethiopian is flat and his thick lips are prominent.

152. London—British Museum—from Tharros. Cf. Smith, *Engraved Gems*, p. 53, no. 181.

Green jasper scarab with a head in profile to right, probably intended to represent an Ethiopian.

153. London—British Museum—from Tharros. Cf. Marshall, *Catalogue of Finger-Rings*, p. 17, no. 81.

Pale gold ring, the thin hoop broadening into an oval bezel, on which is engraved a head probably meant to be an Ethiopian.

154. London—British Museum—from Tharros. Cf. Smith, *Engraved Gems*, p. 52, no. 171, pl. C; Furtwängler, *Antike Gemmen*, I, pl. VII, no. 32; II, p. 34, no. 32; Marshall, *Catalogue of Finger-Rings*, p. 52, no. 292, pl. VIII.

Gold ring with a revolving scarab of green jasper, carved with an elaborate design. The space is filled at the bottom by an animal group, and at the top by three conjoined heads. The middle head is in full front, the others in profile right and left. The profile heads are clearly Ethiopians from their

FIGURE 13.

BRONZE HEAD OF AN AFRICAN.

In the British Museum.

Reproduced from Arndt-Brunn-Bruckmann, *Griechische und Römische Porträts*, pl. 42.

THE ETHIOPIAN TYPE IN THE FOURTH CENTURY   75

short, broad noses and thick lips. The central face, which is distorted in a grin, is called a negro by Smith, but a head of Bes by Furtwängler and Marshall.

155. London—British Museum—Franks Bequest. Cf. Marshall, *Catalogue of Finger-Rings*, p. 223, no. 1456.

Silver ring, gold-plated, with a pointed oval bezel, with an Ethiopian head in profile to left.

While the fourth century, generally speaking, made no advance in the rendering of the racial type on vases or small objects, it produced a portrait head which is extremely fine. Life-sized heads of men with African blood are extremely rare. Only one other deserves to rank with this bronze, a marble head of an Ethiopian from the second century A. D. (No. 289). This head, now in the British Museum, was found among the ruins of the temple of Apollo at Cyrene. It is evident from the fragments of bronze horses found with it that it formed part of a chariot group, and from its dedication in the temple of Apollo it is probable that the man was a victor in the chariot races at Delphi.

156. London—British Museum—from Cyrene. Cf. Smith and Porcher, *Discoveries at Cyrene*, pl. LXVI; Trivier, *Gaz. Arch.*, IV, 1878, p. 60, pl. 8; Rayet, *Monuments de l'Art Antique*, II, pl. 57; Newton, *Guide to Bronze Room*, pp. 49, 12; *Gaz. Arch.*, IX, 1887, p. 397; Smith, *Marbles and Bronzes in the British Museum*, p. 8, pl. 41; Walters, *Catalogue of Bronzes*, p. 34, no. 268; Studniczka, *Kyrene*, p. 5; Brunn-Arndt-Bruckmann, *Griechische u. Römische Porträts*, pls. 41 and 42; Schrader, *Winckelmannspr.*, LX, 1900; Lawrence, *Later Gr. Sc.* pl. 27.

The style of the head appears to be that of the fourth century, with possible Lysippan influences. The growing beard and waving locks of hair are rendered with care, but otherwise there is an absence of realistic detail and any hint of emotion, and the head is notably an idealized portrait. The features are quite regular; the only one suggestive of a strain of negro blood are the lips, which have an unmistakable fullness. The man is a North African of Libya, of a race with features as fine as those of the Cabyles who now inhabit the region. The poise of the head is so noble that it suggested

76 THE NEGRO IN GREEK AND ROMAN CIVILIZATION

to Trivier the idea that here was some Libyan chieftain portrayed in bronze in token of the victory of his splendid horses.

The work is that of a very good artist, though nothing is known of his identity. He had complete mastery over his medium, and even the rendering of the wavy hair, difficult in a material which must be cast from a mould, gave him no difficulty. He achieved the right compromise between fidelity to detail and the effect of the whole. In this respect especially is his handling of his subject in contrast to the treatment of racial types in the next great period of Greek art, namely, the Hellenistic era. Fig. 13.

CHAPTER VI

THE ETHIOPIAN IN THE HELLENISTIC WORLD

After a century in which the Greek world outside of Italy appeared to lose interest in the Ethiopian type (except for the single splendid example whose interest for the sculptor probably lay in some achievement of his career rather than his idealized barbarian features) there was a sudden and new impulse. From the third and second centuries B. C. we have a flood of figurines in terra-cotta, bronze and even marble in which the Ethiopian is delineated with a realism which occasionally crosses the boundary of caricature and the grotesque. All this can only mean some new attitude toward the type which is due to a new influence at work. This is quite patently the founding, the almost mushroom growth and cultural predominance of the city of Alexandria. It would be natural that this city, the most brilliant center of the Hellenistic era, the most completely cosmopolitan, and the one most advantageously placed for the study of African types, should be in large measure responsible for the renewed interest in the Ethiopian.

The sophistication of Alexandria, its social ennui and intellectual godlessness have been wonderfully described by Dickins (*Hellenistic Sculpture,* pp. 27-28).

" The people of Alexandria were noted in the ancient world as scoffers and cynics. Their temper was fiery, their jests were brutal, and reverence of any kind was unknown to them. A cosmopolitan medley of Greek, Macedonian, native Egyptian, Jew, and every nation of the East, they were united only in their utter diversity of point of view and their scepticism of all ideal obligation. To such a people caricature and a love of the grotesque were almost second nature. By the side of the greater art of Alexandria it is easy to discern a lesser art of comic, grotesque, and obscene statuettes of every

78   THE NEGRO IN GREEK AND ROMAN CIVILIZATION

description. . . . In Alexandria above all the grotesque exaggeration of natural defects found its true popularity. The negro, the hunchback, the drunkard, the *crétin* of every kind, became popular artistic models. As if the delineation of youth and beauty were exhausted, the Hellenistic sculptors of Alexandria rushed into the portrayal of disease, of old age and of mutilation in every form. They suffered as much as any modern decadent from 'la nostalgie de la boue.' Here again we must beware of attributing to Alexandria all the grotesque figures of Hellenistic art and all its pieces of most painful naturalism. Pergamum, if not Rhodes, and doubtless Antioch must have played their part in this commonest form of artistic decadence; but we have so much of this work certified as Alexandrian that we are justified in regarding Egypt as its chief and most popular home. Works of this type fall into two classes: the purely grotesque and the extremely naturalistic. . . . We may presume that the demand was primarily foreign and not Greek, though all the skill of Greek sculpture is employed in the faultless execution of many of them."

The foregoing passage well explains why the Ethiopian now appears in genre scenes, studies in ethnographic portraiture, in caricature and the grotesque. The figurines form if not the most important, at least the largest class of negro portraits from antiquity. Schreiber expresses the prevailing opinion so ably seconded by Dickins that Alexandria was the distributing center of the small bronzes. Wace at first believed them to be Campanian, and although he later modified this view, he still refused to believe them Alexandrian because so many are found outside of Egypt. His classification of the figurines is poor, making no distinction between the grotesques and the really artistic figures, and including the life-sized bronze head from Cyrene. Nevertheless their spirit is Alexandrian and the point of their scattered provenance is settled by assuming with Dickins that the demand was foreign. In the case of the Ethiopian bronzes an addi-

THE ETHIOPIAN IN THE HELLENISTIC WORLD   79

tional bit of evidence points to Alexandria. Not only would
Ethiopians be better known in Alexandria than any other
Hellenistic city, but beginning with this period representations of Ethiopians no longer show the curly hair by means
of raised knots but show a new arrangement of the hair in
three or more rows of flat symmetrical curls strongly suggestive of the conventional Egyptian head-dress. This
involved hair arrangement which persists in Roman art is
without doubt as Perdrizet (*Coll. Touquet*, p. 58) points out
the type affected by the Ethiopian butlers of Trimalchio—
"inde subierunt duo Aethiopes *capillati*." [1] Friedländer (p.
225, note to sec. 34) wants to edit *capillati* out of the passage,
but there is no real reason for doing so when it is natural to
think of conspicuous hair in connection with Ethiopians and
the elaborate arrangement on the statuettes explains the passage satisfactorily. These many flat curls recall the groups
of plaited pigtails covering the head of many a small picka-
ninny.

As for the two classes of figurines specified by Dickins, the
grotesque and the extremely naturalistic, the distinction is
hard to make inasmuch as the average white man is inclined
to view humorously a serious realistic portrayal of an African
negro. Nevertheless I find very few of the figurines grotesque, preferring to consider them instances of extreme naturalism. This naturalism in the rendering of the racial types
is entirely compatible with charm as evidenced by a famous
statuette in the Bibliothèque Nationale of an Ethiopian boy
playing the lyre (Fig. 20), the dancing Ethiopian in the
Naples Museum, and the fine statuette in the Metropolitan
Museum in New York (Fig. 19).

The terra-cottas from this period showing Ethiopians seem
to have had other centers of manufacture, and are found principally in Asia Minor and Italy. They were not made at
Tanagra, where the irregular features of the negro did not
attract those craftsmen who concerned themselves chiefly with

---

[1] Cf. Petronius, *Cena Trimalchionis*, sec. 34, Buecheler ed., p. 23.

80   THE NEGRO IN GREEK AND ROMAN CIVILIZATION

the dainty in art. Wace is right in pointing out the popularity of these figurines in Italy and a South Italian factory may
be conjectured for the number brought to light in the lower
part of that peninsula. Perhaps the influence of the Pergamene school, or Antioch, as Dickins suggests, is reflected in
those of Asiatic origin. A few showing genre subjects have
been found even in south Russia and were perhaps an import
from the Asiatic center of manufacture. The Euxine shores
were originally colonized chiefly by Asiatic Greeks and their
commerce with these regions was extensive.

It is not only the Hellenistic bronzes but the baser terra-
cottas which show "all the skill of Greek sculpture in the
faultless execution of many of them." A few are very commonplace, it is true, particularly a group of replicas from
Sicily which are expressionless and stiff. On the other hand,
several are masterly, such as the broken figurine from the
Gréau Collection now in the Berlin Museum, a thick wreath
above a face wearing an expression of pain, and the head in
Berlin found in a Priene house which is virtually a duplicate
of the head of the foregoing figurine. According to Schrader
this head is so realistic that an authority on African tribes,
to whom it was shown, declared that it might easily be a
likeness of a present-day member of one of the least civilized
African tribes. Even finer, as it succeeds in combining an element of pathos with its stark realism, is the tiny figurine
with a vase mouth in the Ashmolean Museum of which there
is a close imitation, if not a replica, in the British Museum
showing a thin little Ethiopian boy asleep, leaning against an
amphora. One of the most interesting is an impudent caricature of the Spinario so beloved by the Greeks, from Priene,
now in Berlin.

The purpose of these terra-cottas, whether decorative or
funerary, is not easy to decide, and probably we would find
instances of both. Froehner believes the Greau Collection
figure in Berlin to have been funerary because of the wreath
in the hair and the wrinkling of the face in what he calls an

THE ETHIOPIAN IN THE HELLENISTIC WORLD 81

expression of pain. But the wrinkles are mere realism and the wreath occurs on far more figures associated with the banquet than with the tomb. On the other hand, three seated figures, one in Bari, one in Berlin, and another in Naples, have the traditional mourning posture of the hand to the head. This recalls the crouching posture of the hand to the head of the seated terra-cottas from the sixth century at Camirus. These were definitely found in tombs and yet the same posture is reproduced on Athenian gems of the sixth and fifth century where it is almost certainly intended to be comic. The Spinario caricature is an outright instance of the comic. Consequently no one rule will apply to all the terra-cottas. Perhaps some were intended to be funerary, others decorative and still others became funerary by accident where favorite decorative or prophylactic objects were buried in the tomb.

The vases of the Hellenistic period are included with the terra-cottas, as several are in reality figurines of the genre type cast hollow with a vase mouth added. They show great variety and no little ingenuity in incorporating the vase mouth as a part of the design. In this respect they outdo the fifth century crocodile vases, though these vases of Sotades are sufficient to refute the statement that in Greek art the search for novel effects and emotional realism is confined to the Hellenistic period. The slave boy with the amphora has been mentioned. Another type probably meant to be humorous shows an Ethiopian crouching down on all fours. In one example he is washing clothes or grinding corn; in another he is filling a vase from a wine skin.

The vases in the form of an Ethiopian's head do not lose ground, in spite of innovations. They differ from the earlier ones in reflecting the new hair arrangement, and are chiefly drinking cups.

CHAPTER VII

TERRA-COTTAS

Figurines and Fragments

157. Athens—Central Museum—Misthos Collection—from Smyrna.
Cf. *Monuments et Memoires, Fondation Piot*, IV, 1897, pl.
XVIII, 2, p. 216; Winter, *Terrakotten*, II, p. 448, no. 5.

Head of Ethiopian with curly hair cut close to his head,
with a wrinkled, retreating forehead, broad nose and thick
lips. Height 0.03 m.

158. Bari—Museo Provinciale—from Monopoli—Inv. no. 1783 a. Cf.
Not. Sc., 1896, p. 546, sec. 3; Winter, *Terrakotten*, II, p. 449,
no. 8.

Figure of a man seated on a rock, his head resting on his
right hand. His pose and expression denote preoccupation
or sadness. To judge his features from the illustration, there
is nothing in his physiognomy especially to indicate an Ethiopian. A barbarian may be intended, though the *Notizie* says
" Moro." A similar figure in the Berlin Museum is painted
brown. Height 0.22 m.

159. Berlin—Königliche Museen—Sabouroff Collection—from Boeotia. Cf. Winter, *Terrakotten*, II, p. 449, no. 8 n; Furtwängler, *Sammlung Sabouroff*, pl. CXXXIX, 2.

Youth seated on a rock, his elbow resting on his left knee
and his left hand supporting his head. His right hand rests
on his right knee. The hands are large in proportion to the
size of the figure. The features are not strongly Ethiopian,
but the figure was painted a dark brown, showing that the
artist intended to show a member of this race. This seems
to be a companion piece to the foregoing as they reverse the
positions of the right and left hand. They were, however,
found far apart.

160. Berlin—Königliche Mussen—Gréau Collection—from Asia
Minor. Cf. Froehner, *Terres Cuites d'Asie de la Coll. Gréau*,
p. 28, pl. 69; Froehner, *Coll. Gréau*, 1891, no. 669; Furtwängler, *Arch. Anz.*, 1892, p. 106, no. 16; Winter, *Terrakotten*, II, p. 448, no. 10.

TERRA-COTTAS

Figurine of an Ethiopian, his arms gone from the shoulder and his legs broken off at the knee. His face has an expression of pain or grief, and his thin body shows above the folds of an *exomis* which is fastened over his left shoulder. On his head is a thick wreath, according to Froehner a funerary crown. This still has traces of color, showing that it was originally painted. The forehead is wrinkled, the lips thick and the nose snub. It closely resembles the head from Priene which follows. This would cast doubt on the idea advanced by Froehner that this statuette was funerary, as the Priene head was not found in a tomb but in a private house with many other terra-cottas. Froehner reads a look of grief into what was intended as naturalistic portraiture. Height 0.145 m.

161. Berlin—Königliche Museen—from Priene. Cf. Wiegand and Schrader, *Priene*, p. 359, fig. 440; Schrader, *Winckelmanns-program*, Berlin, LX, 1900, pp. 23 and 36; Winter, *Terrakotten*, II, p. 448, no. 4.

Head of an Ethiopian, crowned with a wreath of flowers, found with many other terra-cottas in a house in Priene. It is not a caricature but an extremely naturalistic portrait of an African of the lowest type of intelligence. Schrader says that an authority on African tribes to whom it was shown stated without hesitation that a woman was meant, and that it might easily be the picture of a present day member of one of the least civilized Central African tribes.

The handling of detail and the effect produced are masterly. The thick, coarse, half open lips are in startling contrast to the elaborate garland which hangs down on either side of the face. There are remains of dark brown color on hair and flesh. Height 0.07 m.

162. Berlin—Königliche Museen 8626—from Priene. Cf. Wiegand, *Priene*, p. 357, figs. 434-435; Winter, *Terrakotten*, II, p. 448, no. 1; *Jb.*, XXIX, 1914, p. 24, n. 3.

A figurine caricaturing the famous "Spinario" as an Ethiopian. His forehead is wrinkled and his eyes have an expression of pain. His nose is short and broad at the base,

84 THE NEGRO IN GREEK AND ROMAN CIVILIZATION

and while his lips are not large, a grotesque effect is given by his exaggerated puffed-out cheeks. He wears a cap on his head, and some drapery fastened up over one shoulder. His body is somewhat dwarfed, with head large in proportion. Height 0.165 m.

163. Berlin—Königliche Museen no. 7597—from Asia Minor. Cf. Winter, *Terrakotten*, II, p. 448, no. 7.

Head of an Ethiopian or barbarian, with short, broad nose and thick lips. Height 0.04 m.

164. Berlin—Königliche Museen, no. 6968, formerly Kommos Coll., Athens—from the Cyrenaica. Cf. Winter *Terrakotten*, II, p. 448, no. 6.

Head of a barbarian or an Ethiopian with a long beard. The lips are thick, the nose broken off. Height 0.055 m.

165. Constantinople Museum—from Assos. Cf. Winter, *Terrakotten*, II, p. 448, no. 9.

Fragment of an Ethiopian's head, the cranium missing. The hair is in long locks, but the negro blood is evident in the broad nose, thick lips and wrinkled forehead. Height 0.035 m.

166. Cyprus Museum—from Citium, Kamelarga site. Cf. Myres and Richter, *Cyprus Museum*, p. 155, no. 5549.

Terra-cotta head of an Ethiopian woman broken from a figurine, found with other terra-cottas in a sanctuary, probably that of Artemis. Height 0.08 m.

167. Gréau Collection. Cf. Froehner, *Terres Cuites d'Asie de la Collection Julien Gréau*, vol. I, p. 70, no. 5; vol. II, pl. 83.

Head of an Ethiopian with curly hair, low, wrinkled, scowling forehead, flat nose (partly gone), and thick lips, the lower one protruding.

168. Gréau Collection—from Tarentum. Cf. Froehner, *Collection Gréau*, 1891, p. 148, no. 257; Winter, *Terrakotten*, II, p. 449, footnote.

Mould for a terra-cotta bust of an Ethiopian boy, his left arm raised. Height 0.08 m.

169. London—British Museum—from lower Italy. Cf. Winter, *Terrakotten*, II, p. 449, no. 8 b; Walters, *Catalogue of Terracottas*, p. 311, no. D 86.

TERRA-COTTAS 85

Ethiopian with curly hair and characteristic features, seated on a rock, about to write on a scroll. Except for the writing, the pose recalls the seated terra-cottas in the Bari and Berlin Museums. Height 8 in.

170. London—British Museum—from Italy. Cf. Walters, *Catalogue of Terracottas*, p. 310, D 84.

Ethiopian boxer, with *caestus* on both hands and a loin cloth about his waist. His features are coarse and he is partly bald. He leans back, with his arms out in front of him. Height 10⅜ in.

171. London—British Museum—from Italy. Cf. Walters, *Catalogue of Terracottas*, p. 311, no. D 85.

Mate to the foregoing figure, with left foot advanced and right arm raised as if to strike. His face is more youthful than his companion's, and there are traces of dark color still visible on it. Height 9⅜ in.

172. London—British Museum—from Italy. Cf. Walters, *Catalogue of Terracottas*, p. 365, no. D 361.

Life-sized mask of an Ethiopian evidently intended to be worn, as the mouth, nostrils, and pupils of the eyes are pierced through. Each ear has been pierced with a hole, which was probably intended for the cord which held the mask in place. The hair is in clusters of curls, the nose flat, and the mouth grinning, with the upper row of teeth indicated. Height 8⅞ in.

173. Naples—Museo Nazionale 6855 (4704)—from Capua. Cf. Winter, *Terrakotten*, II, p. 449, 8 c.

Figure seated on a rock. Similar to that from Bari. His head is resting on his hand. Height 0.21 m.

174. Odessa Museum—from Olbia. *Inventarkatalog*, IV, 39; Cf. Von Stern, *Jh. Oest. Arch. Inst.*, VII, 1904, p. 201, no. 2.

Unpublished terra-cotta head of an Ethiopian woman, painted glossy black.

175. Odessa Museum. Cf. Von Stern, *Jh. Oest. Arch. Inst.*, VII, 1904, p. 201, no. 1.

Fragment of a terra-cotta pendant in the form of an Ethiopian's head.

86   THE NEGRO IN GREEK AND ROMAN CIVILIZATION

176. Paris—Louvre—from Aegae (Aeolis).   Cf. Pottier-Reinach,
Les Terres Cuites de Myrina, no. 687; Winter, Terrakotten,
II, p. 448, no. 12.

Head of an Ethiopian inclined toward the left shoulder.
Ht. 0.035 m.

177. Paris—Louvre no. 335—from the necropolis of Myrina.   Cf.
Pottier-Reinach, Myrina, II, p. 473, pl. XLVI, no. 2; Winter,
Terrakotten, II, p. 448, no. 12.

An Ethiopian or barbarian slave, carrying a dish on his
up-raised left hand (balanced as a modern waiter balances a
tray), and an oenochoe in his right hand, which hangs by
his side. He wears a loin cloth about his waist. His wavy
hair is long and hangs about his neck, his eyes are set far
apart, his nose is short and his thick lips protrude somewhat.
Ht. 0.17 in.

178. Paris—Louvre—from Smyrna.   Cf. Winter, Terrakotten, II,
p. 448, 5.

Head of an Ethiopian with curly hair, the flesh painted
black, similar to the head in the Central Museum, Athens
(no. 157, above).

179. Leningrad—Hermitage—from Cimmeria.   Cf. Stephani, Compte
Rendu, 1868, p. 61, no. 8; Atlas, pl. II, no. 3; Schneider,
Jb. Kunst. Samml., III, 1885, p. 7, n. 1.

A nude Ethiopian youth, found with a group of the Niobids
in terra-cotta. He has sunk to his knees and his head is
thrown backwards. His right arm, which was evidently
up-raised, has been broken off. His left hand holds the
remains of a sack which was thrown over his left shoulder.
This hunting sack is evidence that the Ethiopian was
intended as an attendant of the sons of Niobe who were killed
while out hunting.

This figurine is of especial interest because, although a
genre type, it is connected with mythology. The portrayal
of Ethiopians in connection with mythology is usually confined to vases.

180. Syracuse Museum—from Ortygia.   Cf. Kekulé von Stradonitz,
Terrakotten von Sicilien, pl. LI, no. 1.

Figurine with legs apart. The position is a seated one.

TERRA-COTTAS 87

It has been put together from fragments. The hands on the knees. Figure hollow. Lower legs cast solid. Heads modeled separately and then fastened on. In this way one mould head could be used for several figures. The same mould is used for the heads of the other figures.

The head inclines forward. The hair is only moderately curly. The forehead is excessively wrinkled between the eyes, which are wide open and rectangular in outline. The nose rises from a depression between the eyes, and is broad at the extremity. The lips are thick, protruding and tightly closed. The unusually large eyes are characteristic of the modern Nubian. Ht. 0.24 m.

181. Syracuse Museum. Cf. Kekulé, *Terrakotten von Sicilien*, pl. LI, no. 2, p. 80; Winter, *Terrakotten*, II, p. 449, no. 7.

The hands are held in front of the breast. The legs are crossed at the ankles. Put together from fragments. Ht. 0.24 m.

182. Syracuse Museum. Cf. Kekulé, *Terrakotten von Sicilien*, pl. LI, no. 3, p. 80.

Figurine similar to the above except that the arms and a portion of the right breast are broken off. A streak of black color is still visible in the face and hair, making the identification as an Ethiopian certain. Height 0.24 m. Put together from fragments.

183. Toronto—The Royal Ontario Museum of Archaeology—unpublished.

Terra-cotta head of an Ethiopian with flat nose, thick parted lips and high cheek bones. The racial type is caricatured.

184. Trieste—Museo Civico—from Tarentum. Cf. Winter, *Terrakotten*, II, p. 449, no. 2.

Figure in the traditional crouching position, asleep. His thick lips are the only evidence of negro blood in his physiognomy, but the pose is the conventional one for the Ethiopian slave. Part of the right arm and right leg are missing. Ht. 0.09 in.

88 THE NEGRO IN GREEK AND ROMAN CIVILIZATION

185. Trieste—Museo Civico—from Tarentum. Cf. Winter, *Terra-kotten*, II, p. 449, no. 6.

Standing figurine, wearing a loin-cloth and holding castanets in his hand. His slightly parted, thick lips and his hair, in conventional rows of flat curls, indicate Ethiopian blood. Ht. 0.145.

VASES

186. Athens—National Museum. Cf. Nicole, *Catalogue des Vases Peints*, p. 283, no. 229.

Ointment vase in the form of an Ethiopian's head, from the Hellenistic period. In the hair is an ivy wreath. Greenish clay with black glaze.

187. Athens—National Museum. Cf. Nicole, *Catalogue des Vases Peints*, p. 283, no. 1330.

Similar vase in the form of an Ethiopian's head.

188. Athens—National Museum. Cf. Nicole, *Catalogue des Vases Peints*, p. 283, no. 1331.

Similar vase in the form of an Ethiopian's head, similar to the preceding.

189. Baltimore—Coll. of Professor D. M. Robinson—bought in Tarentum.

This is an unpublished drinking cup or pitcher in the form of an Ethiopian's head. His neck serves as a base, and a simple cylindrical spout with a trefoil opening inside rises from the top of his head. A flat channeled handle curves from the back of the spout to the back of his head. Only the face and front of the hair are modeled, the clay at the back of the head being left smooth. There is an incised inscription at the back of the Ethiopian's neck, near the bottom of the vase, AA. Possibly this is only a decoration and not meant to be an inscription. The entire surface of the vase was covered with a black glaze, much of which still remains. The vase was made in two sections, the modelled front and plain back, and then joined together.

The hair of the Ethiopian is in three rows of spiral curls over his forehead and ears, and fits like a cap about his forehead, which is deeply wrinkled. The eyebrows are heavy, and

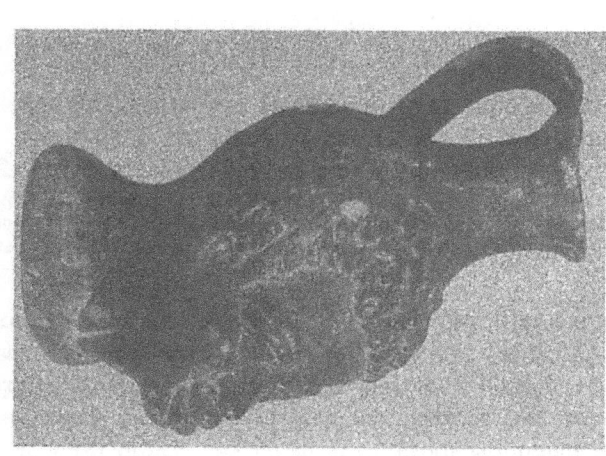

FIGURE 14.
PITCHER.
In Collection of David M. Robinson, Baltimore, Md.

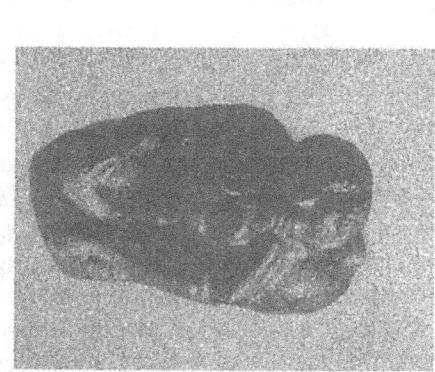

FIGURE 15.
THIRD CENTURY B.C. NEGRO.
In Munich.
By Courtesy of Professor Sieveking.

TERRA-COTTAS 89

are rendered by means of incised lines, herring-bone pattern, in the clay. The eyes are wide open, the iris shown by an incised circle, with a raised dot in the center to represent the pupil. The nose, rising from a depression between the eyes, broadens at the base almost to the width of the mouth. The lips are very thick and protruding, and are parted to show the white teeth. There is a prominence about the jaw structure which renders the profile ape-like in effect. The ears are set very low in the head, in line with the mouth. The throat is drawn and tense, and the muscles stand out sharply. Height of entire vase 5½ in. (0.135 m.); height from base to top of Ethiopian's head 4⅛ in. (0.105 m.). Fig. 14.

190 London—British Museum—Castellani Coll.—from Capua. Cf. Walters, *Catalogue of Vases*, IV, p. 262, G 154

Ascus in the form of a crouching Ethiopian boy, asleep. His right leg is drawn up in front of him, and his head rests on his hands, which clasp his right knee. He is nude except for a garment tied around his throat. An amphora at his back forms the spout of the vase. Early Hellenistic work, similar to the vase in the Ashmolean Museum, Oxford.

191. Naples—National Museum—Museo Borbonico. Cf. Heydemann, *Museo Nazionale*, p. 7, no. 185.

Small black vase with the head of an Ethiopian in relief.

192. New Haven—Yale University—Stoddard Collection. Cf. Baur, *Catalogue*, p. 227, no. 455, fig. 102.

Vase of light brown clay in the form of an Ethiopian, who crouches on all fours, animal fashion, filling a vase from a wine skin. Over his head and shoulders is a panther's skin fastened under his chin. The trumpet-shaped mouth of the vase projects from the middle of his back. Early Hellenistic period. Ht. 3⅜ in.

193. New York—Metropolitan Museum—Morgan Collection—formerly Gréau Collection. Cf. Froehner, *Verrerie Antique*, p. 267, no. 56, vol. V, pl. 335.

Fragment of a vase in the form of a grotesque Ethiopian's head. The hair is indicated by three rows of conventional curls. The forehead is low and wrinkled, and the eye-brows,

90   THE NEGRO IN GREEK AND ROMAN CIVILIZATION

modelled in the clay, are heavy and close together. The nose is short, broad and flat, and the lower lip thick and protruding, disclosing a row of teeth. The beard is indicated by crescent-shaped incisions in the clay.

194. Odessa Museum. *Inventarkatalog,* IV, 243; Cf. Stern, *Jh. Oest. Arch. Inst.,* VII, 1904, p. 201, no. 3.

Unpublished vase in the form of a crouching Ethiopian painted black. The expression of the face is sad, like that of a bronze statuette from Chalon-sur-Saône in the Bibliothèque Nationale (below, no. 214).

195. Odessa Museum. Cf. *Terracotten des Odessaer Museums,* II, pl. XII, 1; Stern, *Jh. Oest. Arch. Inst.,* VII, 1904, p. 201, no. 4.

Vase in the form of a negro's head, of red clay.

196. Odessa Museum—from Olbia.

Ointment vase in the form of a negro's head.

197. Oxford—Ashmolean Museum—from Tarentum. Cf. Evans, *J. H. S.,* 1886, pp. 37-38, pl. LXIV; Lawrence, *Later Greek Sculpture,* pl. 3.

"A little negro slave boy coiled up fast asleep under an amphora against which he huddles as if for shelter from the Bora. The characteristic features of the race are admirably rendered, including the woolly hair, protuberant forehead, thick lips and indescribable nigger grin. The backbone, ribs and muscles of the half-starved little form are indicated with anatomic precision and even the dolichocephalic skull and disproportionately long arms of the negroid type are faithfully reproduced. This surprising accuracy of detail, however, is not won at the expense of the general effect of the figure, which for life-like realism and true pathos is probably without a rival amongst Greek terra-cottas " (Evans). Ht. 2.5 in.

The vase is similar to the ascus in the British Museum and Evans says that a figure of black stone spotted with green, identical in attitude except that the child was crying, was sold in Paris, the present ownership being unknown. Also in the Ashmolean Museum (1922. 205) is an ascus from Boeotian

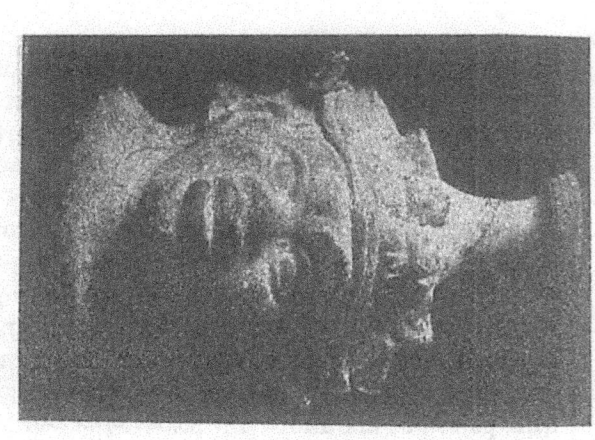

FIGURE 16.
THIRD CENTURY B.C. VASE.
In Munich.
By Courtesy of Professor Sieveking.

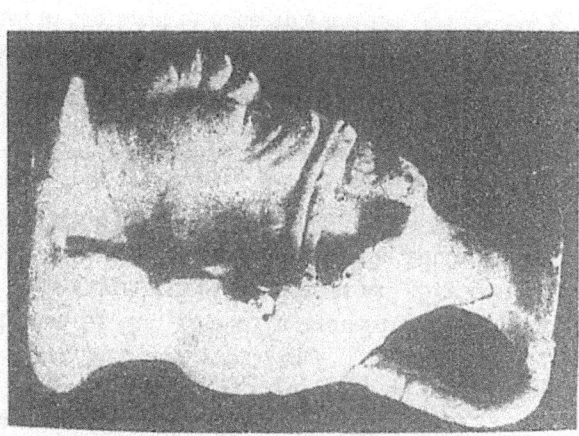

FIGURE 17.
PROFILE OF FIGURE 16.

TERRA-COTTAS 91

Thebes in the form of a negro boy bent over to the ground. We reproduce in Fig. 15 an unpublished example in Munich in the Pinakothek dating from the third century B. C.

198. Pourtalès Collection. Cf. Panofka, *Cabinet Pourtales*, p. 115, pl. XXX.

Vase in the form of an Ethiopian boy on his knees, bending forward as if washing some object in a stream. The vase mouth projects from the lower part of his back, and a handle connects it with the middle of his spine. His nose is snub, his lips thick, his hair moderately curly and his whole face childish. Possibly he is grinding corn.

199. Rome—Villa Giulia Museum. Cf. Della Seta, *Museo di Villa Giulia*, p. 336, no. 25876.

Guttus decorated with the head of an Ethiopian in relief on the top.

200. Vienna—Kunsthistorisches Museum—from Anthedon (?). Cf. Schneider, *Jh. Oest. Arch. Inst.*, IX, 1906, p. 321, fig. 75, pl. II; Schneider, *Arch. Anz.*, VII, 1892, p. 118, no. 142. Ducati, *Storia della Ceramica Greca*, II, p. 527, fig. 402.

Vase in the form of an Ethiopian's head, the features caricatured. The forehead is low and wrinkled, the nose snub and the lips exaggeratedly thick. The woolly hair is surmounted by an ivy wreath. Hair in rows of conventional spiral curls in the Egyptian fashion. In it is a taenia which lies over the forehead bow-shaped and falls behind the ears on either side. Scanty traces of white on teeth and of blue on the wreath and of pink on lips and cheeks. There is a simple cylindrical spout at the top of the head, a twisting handle connecting its brim with the back of the Ethiopian's head. In comparison with the life-like heads of the sixth and fifth centuries this is an asymmetrical monstrosity. Third Century Work. Ht. 0.15 m.

In Munich is a very similar unpublished vase which we reproduce in Figs. 16 and 17.

201. Sold in New York—Chinielowski Coll.—from Olbia. Cf. Sale Catalogue, Auction Feb. 20, 1922.

Vase shaped like an Ethiopian's head, painted black. Ht. 7¼ in.

CHAPTER VIII

HELLENISTIC BRONZES

Individually more artistic than the terra-cottas are the bronze statuettes which found their inspiration in Alexandria. This guarded expression is used inasmuch as it seems inadvisable to attempt a more subtle classification into Greek, Graeco-Roman or Roman. It is possible that some are Roman —indeed their provenance places them clearly in the Roman era—but such are either Alexandrian in spirit or can be shown to be excellent copies of Greek originality. Certain types of objects can be shown to be Roman work, as they all betray a certain attitude toward the Ethiopian type which will be shown to be the psychology of Rome and not of Greece. Such objects will be treated separately under Rome. But the statuettes are definitely Greek in spirit. Their realism is softened with Greek charm or spiced with Alexandrian insolence; it is not the photographic and often inert realism of Rome. This chapter, then, covers statuettes definitely Alexandrian, others whose Greek or Roman origin is disputed by authorities equally worthy of consideration, a few from Roman times and places but with Greek parallels or ancestry and one or two for which the *ex cathedra* pronouncement of museum catalogues must be accepted.

Many more of these bronzes come from Egypt than do the terra-cottas. A few are masterly and all deserve fuller mention. They are as follows:

BRONZE STATUETTES

202. Arolsen Museum. Cf. Gaedechens, *Die Antiken Museum zu Arolsen*, p. 108, no. 444; Friederichs-Wolters, *Gipsabguesse antiker Bildwerke*, p. 698, no. 1785.

Statuette of an Ethiopian boy seated on the ground with his left leg drawn close to him and his right drawn up in front. His head rests on his hands which clasp his right knee.

HELLENISTIC BRONZES 93

His eyes are closed as if in sleep. The pose is traditional and occurs on terra-cottas and gems from the sixth century on.

203. Athens—Polytechnikon—Demetriou Collection—from Alexandria. Cf. Puchstein, *Ath. Mitth.*, VII, 1882, p. 14, no. 332; Schreiber, *Ath. Mitth.*, X, 1885, p. 383, pl. XI, 2; Reinach, *Répertoire de Statuaire*, II, p. 562, no. 4; Wace, *B. S. A.*, X, 1903-4, p. 107, E 5.

Statuette of an Ethiopian seated on the ground, asleep, a tray of fruit in front of him and a tiny monkey on his right shoulder. He is probably, as Schreiber suggests, an Alexandrian fruit vender taking his siesta by going to sleep at his post, with his wares in front of him. He is treated in strong caricature. His position is the traditional crouching one, his head resting on his hands, which clasp his right knee. His body is miserably thin, and the bony structure of his face stands out prominently. The hair is in rows of conventional locks like flower petals, the nose is short and broad and the thick lips are slightly parted. Height 0.05 m.

204. Berlin—Königliche Museen—Antiquarium no. 7456—from Egypt. Cf. *Arch. Zeit.*, XXXVIII, 1880, p. 39; Wace, *B. S. A.*, X, 1903-4, p. 107, E 1.

Young Ethiopian wearing trousers, his hands behind his back.

205. Bologna Museum. Cf. Gozzadini, *Di Ulteriore Scoperte nell' antica necropoli a Marzabotto nel Bolognese*, pl. XII, 6 c, comp. 38; Schneider, *Jb. Kunst. Samml.*, III, 1885, p. 7, n. 8.

Bronze statuette of an Ethiopian youth carrying an amphora on his shoulder.

206. Courtot Collection. Cf. Reinach, *Répertoire de Statuaire*, IV, p. 353, no. 5.

Statuette of a standing Ethiopian who holds a bird in his right hand. His hair is in wavy locks, his nose broad and his lips thick. He is heavy in build, and does not show the emaciated thinness characteristic of most negro portraits.

207. Deutsch-Altenburg Museum—from Carnuntum. Cf. Schneider, *Jh. Oest. Arch. Inst.*, IX, 1906, pp. 323-4, pl. III; Kubitschek, *Führer durch Carnuntum*, p. 54; Bulle, *Der Schoene Mensch*, p. 673, 145; Reinach, *Répertoire de Statuaire*, IV, p. 354, no. 1; Perdrizet, *Collection Fouquet*, p. 57.

94 THE NEGRO IN GREEK AND ROMAN CIVILIZATION

Bronze statuette of a negro usually interpreted as a dancer caught at one of the wildest moments of his dance. The left foot and left hand are gone, but the twist of the body indicates that he was momentarily poised on the toe of the foot which is missing, his right leg drawn up preparatory to the next leap of the dance. His head is thrown back and there is an expression of frenzy on his face. This is the traditional interpretation of the pose. But the left leg does not look as if it were maintaining the weight of the body, even momentarily, and the figure is probably swimming. The head is thrown back as if to keep it clear of the water. The expression of frenzy may mean that he is escaping from a crocodile.

His hair is in three rows of spiral curls; his forehead is deeply wrinkled. The eye-balls are inset in silver, with a hollow left to indicate the pupil. The nose rises from a depression between the eyes and broadens at the end. His mouth is large and his thick lips are parted in the abandon of the moment. The finger-nails are rendered with fidelity.

Fouquet says that from its provenance the statue can not be earlier than the first century A. D. It is true that it can not have been taken to Carnuntum earlier than this date, though that does not prove that it was not made earlier. Its pose is that of a figure in Lisbon, but the Lisbon figure is of much poorer workmanship. Either the Lisbon figure is a copy of this one or both are copies, one excellent and one poor, of an Alexandrian figure. The use of silver inlay for the eyes is not confined to either period, but occurs on well attested examples from both.

The figure has more life and motion than any other classical statuette of the Ethiopian type. Height (in its present state) 0.085 m. Fig. 18.

208. Dortmund—Collection of Dr. Albrecht Jorden—from Sparta. Cf. Dressel-Milchhoeffer, *Ath. Mitth.*, II, 1877, p. 361, no. 139; Schneider, *Jb. Kunst. Samml.*, III, 1885, p. 8; Friederichs-Wolters, *Gipsabguesse Antiker Bildwerke*, p. 698, no. 1785; Blümner, *Führer . . . Universität Zurich*, p. 110, no. 990; Reinach, *Répertoire de Statuaire*, III, p. 158, no. 10.

Boy seated on the ground in the usual crouching position,

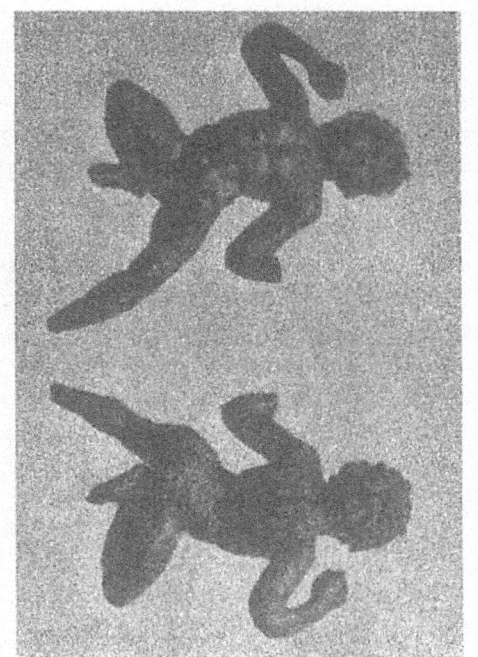

FIGURE 18.
BRONZE STATUETTE FROM CARNUNTUM.

asleep, his head resting on his right knee. The original publication does not call him a negro, but in subsequent references he is called without comment a negro. In the illustration available it is difficult to see any traces of the Ethiopian in his physiognomy, though his pose is the traditional seated posture familiar among statuettes of Ethiopians from an early period. This figure is more widely known than many better ones because it has been reproduced by casts in the Berlin and Zurich museums. The left arm and right foot are missing. It is included here because it is commonly known as an Ethiopian. Height 0.056 m.

209. Fouquet Collection—Bronzes Grecs—from Egypt. Cf. Perdrizet,
Coll. Fouquet, p. 57, no. 93, pl. XXV.

Ethiopian boy crouching down on all fours, with head thrown back and turned to the right. The left arm is gone at the elbow, the left leg at the knee and the right arm at the shoulder. The suggestions offered by Perdrizet in explanation of the pose are (1) that he is undergoing punishment (which is entirely out of harmony with the mischievous expression of his face, and for which there is no parallel among representations of Ethiopians) or (2) that he is stalking some prey, such as a bird's nest (which is admissible from pose and expression). It is more probable that like the Carnuntum and Lisbon figures he is swimming, as his legs are drawn up in swimming position, and what remains of his arms indicates that they also would be correctly placed for this interpretation. His head is held up as if to keep it clear of the water. Perhaps he is diving after coins. He has a parallel in the busts of diving negroes in the British Museum, and the Bibliothèque Nationale. His hair is in regular rows of curls, his eyes have hollows to represent the pupils, his nose is short and very broad at the base and his lips are thick, the lower one prominent. He wears a short tunic fastened about his waist. The left arm is gone at the elbow, the left leg at the knee and the right arm at the shoulder. The expression is full of mischief and lifelike, and this little figure is one of the most interesting of the genre portraits of negroes. Length 0.102 m.

96 THE NEGRO IN GREEK AND ROMAN CIVILIZATION

210. Leipzig—Theodor Graf Collection—from Egypt. Cf. Schreiber, *Arch. Anz.*, V, 1890, p. 157, fig. 8; Wace, *B. S. A.*, X, 1903-4, p. 107, no. 9.

Nude female figurine in stiff erect pose, the legs close together. The arms are missing and there are sockets where they were intended to be fastened to the figure. The hair is in conventional rows of flat locks, radiating from the top of the head as a center. The face is very round, with low forehead, nose short but not negroid, and thick full lips. Schreiber calls her an "Aegypterin," Wace a negress. Height 0.21 m.

211. Lisbon—Bucelles Osorio. Cf. *Arch. Portugues*, VIII, 1903, p. 304; Reinach, *Répertoire de Statuaire*, IV, p. 354, no. 3.

Bronze figure in the exact pose of the dancing Ethiopian from Carnuntum. Most of both arms is missing. The head, however, while bent in the same way, shows different features, the hair being conventionalized, and the expression of the face being softened from frenzy to passivity. The provenance of the figure is not given, but its relation to the other is indisputable. Its poorer workmanship would indicate a copy.

212. Naples—Museo Nazionale, no. 5486—from Herculaneum. Cf. Roux et Barre, VI, p. 199, pl. 104, 1 and 3; *Bronzi d'Ercolano*, II, p. 361, pl. XV; Reinach, *Répertoire de Statuaire*, II, p. 563, nos. 4-5; Wace, *B. S. A.*, X, 1903-4, p. 107, no. 8; Calza, *Jour. Rom. St.*, V, 1915, p. 169, n. 3.

Dancing Ethiopian with a short chiton fastened over his left shoulder. The dance is not a furious one such as may be shown in the Carnuntum and Lisbon bronzes but a slower, more graceful measure. The dancer's right arm is extended in front of him, with his left drawn back and bent at the elbow. He balances on his left foot, with his right foot poised in the air back of him. His head is bent back and turned toward the right. The hair is in rows of locks, and the broad nose and thick lips attest the negro origin. The head is large in proportion to the body, perhaps indicating a dwarf.

213. New York—Metropolitan Museum. Cf. Richter, *Bulletin of the Metr. Mus.*, XV, 1920, p. 109; and XVI, 1921, pp. 33-35, fig. 3.

Statuette of an Ethiopian, nude except for an elaborately

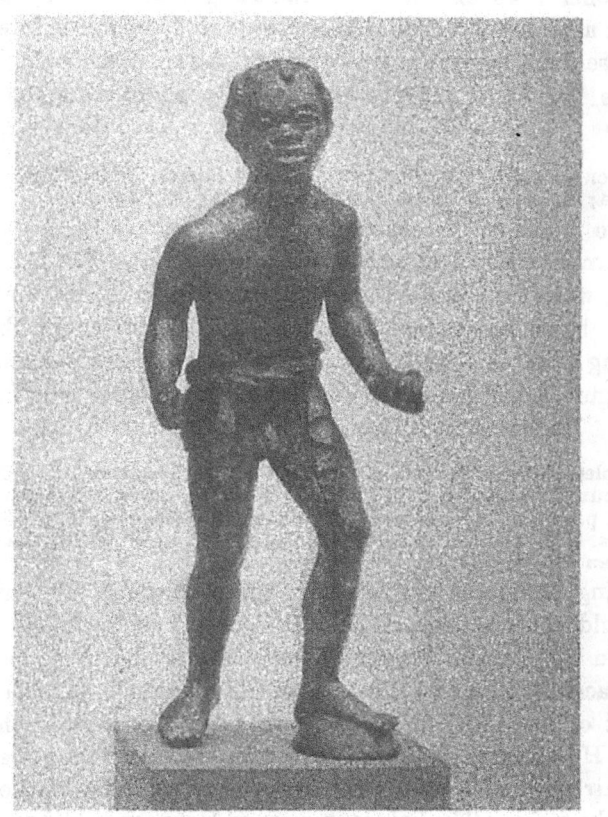

FIGURE 19.

BRONZE NEGRO BOY.

In Metropolitan Museum of Art.

twisted mantle about his waist, revealing the soft modeling of the flesh. He carries some object in his hands and leans forward in what Miss Richter calls a walking attitude. This seems unlikely, as both knees are bent at more of an angle than would be normal in ordinary walking. It may be a posture in some barbaric dance, in which case the objects in his hands would be castanets, or he may be an athlete, and his position one of combat. There is a tenseness about the figure which the walking interpretation does not explain. It is possible that he is holding reins in his hand and driving, from the way his foot is braced.

The hair is in long spiral curls against the head, with a single curl in the middle of the long retreating forehead. The hollow eye-sockets were originally filled with some substance, probably silver, which has fallen away. The nose, rising from a depression between the eyes, is very broad at the base, and the slightly parted lips are thick, the lower one protruding. It is a fine example of Hellenistic art. Height $7\frac{3}{16}$ in. (0.183 m.) Fig. 19.

214. Paris—Bibliothèque Nationale—Caylus Coll. from Châlon-sur-Saône. Cf. Caylus, *Receuil*, vol. VII, p. 280, pl. LXXXI, nos. 3-5, du Mersan, *Histoire du Cabinet des Medailles*, p. 69, no. 207; *Monumenti dell'Inst.*, IV, pl. 20 b; *Annali*, XVII, 1845, pp. 283 sqq; Panofka, *Delphi u. Melaine*, Berlin, *Winckelmanns program*, IX, p. 15, n. 73; Chabouillet, *Catalogue du Cabinet des Medailles*, no. 3078; Schreiber, *Ath. Mitth.*, X, 1885, p. 395; Schneider, *Jb. Kunst. Samml.*, III, 1885, p. 8; Rayet, *Monuments de l'art antique*, II, 6, pl. XIII; Heydemann, *Pariser Antiken*, p. 69, no. 9; Babelon, *Le Cabinet des Antiques*, pp. 151-3, pl. XLVI; Pottier-Reinach, *Myrina*, pp. 474 and 485; Schrader, *Winckelmannsf. Prog.*, Berlin, 60, 1900, p. 16; Wace, *B.S.A.*, X, 1903-4, p. 107; Collignon-Baumgarten, *Griech. Skulptur.*, II, fig. 294; Reinach, *Répertoire de Statuaire*, II, p. 561, no. 4; Babelon-Blanchet, *Catalogue des Bronzes*, pp. 439-440, no. 1009; Bulle, *Der Schöne Mensch*, pp. 145-6, no. 77, fig. 29, pl. 77.

This is the best known and probably the finest statuette of an Ethiopian. It came to light in the year 1763 at Châlon-sur-Saône in a chest, together with some other bronzes of evident Roman origin. The condition of the chest showed that it had not been buried long, though the mystery of its burial

98   THE NEGRO IN GREEK AND ROMAN CIVILIZATION

was never solved. The grace of the figure and the skill of
the work are the reasons for its assignment by all to the
Hellenistic period, notwithstanding that the rest of the
bronzes were Roman.

The statuette portrays an Ethiopian boy standing with his
slim body bent gracefully at the waist, his left arm held in
front of him as if supporting some object on his shoulder and
his mouth open as if singing. It seems reasonably certain
that his left hand held in place a *trigonon* which rested
against his shoulder, and from which he is drawing the notes
with his right hand, which is placed as if about to pick the
strings. The dreamy sadness of his expression and the
"langueur" of his pose give, as Collignon suggests, the illusion that he is actually singing some sad song of his home-
land. The interpretation of Wace that he is a hawker crying
his wares seems untenable, not only from the pose and the
expression of the face, but because such hawkers are generally
portrayed in caricature. The interpretation of Caylus and
Heydemann, that he is wounded and twisting with pain, is
not accepted by the others.

While the characteristic Ethiopian features are present,
particularly in the profile, they are treated so that the effect is
pleasing. The hair is arranged in formal stages of curls—
the Alexandrian style—the forehead is wrinkled, the nose is
not coarse, and the thickness of the lips is moderated. The
upper row of teeth is indicated, and the eyes are inset in silver, with a hollow to indicate the pupil. The work is generally assigned to Alexandria. The height is only 0.20 m.,
but the work is so excellent that photographs give the illusion
of a large statue. Fig. 20.

215. Paris—Bibliothèque Nationale. Cf. du Mersan, *Histoire du
Cabinet des Medailles*, p. 63, no. 133; Chamouillet, *Catalogue*,
no. 3079; Babelon-Blanchet, *Catalogue des Bronzes*, p. 440, no.
1010; Reinach, *Répertoire de Statuaire*, II, p. 563; Wace,
B. S. A., X, 1903-4, p. 107, no. 7.

Ethiopian boy, standing, clad in a tunic which covers him
from his neck to his knees and which is drawn in at the waist

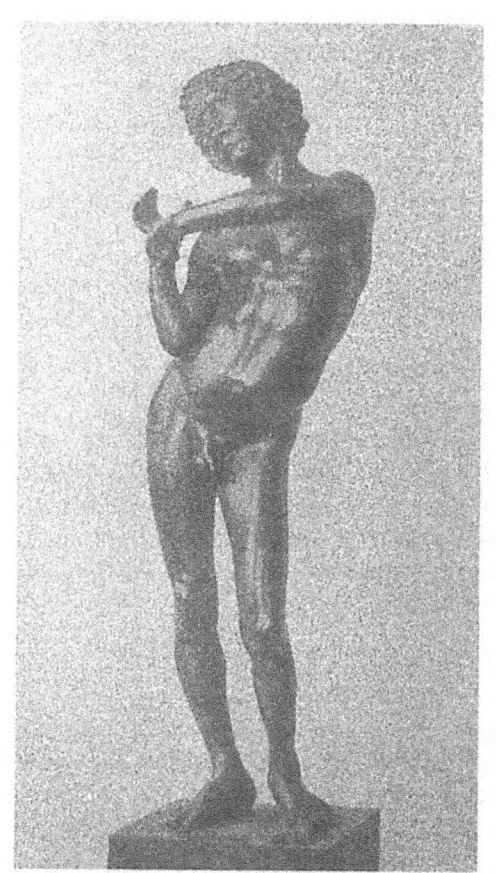

FIGURE 20.

A BRONZE ETHIOPIAN BOY.

In Paris.

HELLENISTIC BRONZES 99

by a girdle tied in front. His pose would indicate that he is pulling some heavy object toward him, or holding reins to check horses, as his left foot and left shoulder are thrust forward, with his head inclined away from them. The arms are entirely gone, though there is an opening in the tunic on either side which shows where they emerged.

The hair is in the conventional rows of flat locks; the eyeballs are inset in silver; the nose is squat at the base; the lips are thick. The work is probably Alexandrian. Ht. 0.175 m.

216. Paris—Louvre. Cf. Reinach, *Répertoire de Statuaire*, II, p. 561, no. 8.

Ethiopian standing, his hands behind his back, his body bent as in the Châlon-sur-Saône statuette. His hair is curly and his lower lip protrudes in exaggerated fashion.

217. St. Germain—found at Rheims; Cf. Reinach, *Répertoire de Statuaire*, II, p. 561, no. 5; Reinach, *Catalogue du Musée de Saint-Germain*, p. 125.

Statuette of a negro boy standing with the weight on the left foot, his body bent at the waist in the pose of the preceding figure but turned in the opposite direction. His right arm is missing and his left is extended in front of him with palm upwards. His head inclines toward the left, his hair is in curls and his lips are thick.

218. Stuttgart—Staatssammlung—from Herbrechtingen. Cf. Mayer, *Arch. Anzeiger*, V, 1890, p. 97-98; Reinach, *Répertoire de Statuaire*, II, p. 561.

219. Toulouse. Cf. Reinach, *Répertoire de Statuaire*, II, p. 561.

Ethiopian standing with his weight on his right foot. Both arms are gone. The head is turned to the right, and shows curly hair, broad nose, and thick lips.

220. Vienna—Kaiserl. Königl. Oesterr. Museum. Cf. Schneider, *Jb. Kunst. Samml.*, III, 1885, p. 3; Schneider, *Arch. Anzeiger*, VII, 1892, p. 50; Reinach, *Répertoire de Statuaire*, II, p. 562, no. 2.

Bronze figurine in relief style, of an Ethiopian boy crouching down with his head on his right knee, asleep. His woolly hair is indicated by large round dots, and his thick lips are

100 THE NEGRO IN GREEK AND ROMAN CIVILIZATION

parted. The exact provenance of this figure is unknown, but it is supposed to have come from Greece. He must be the earliest of the series and possibly dates from a previous period because of the technique of the hair.

221. Weimar—Goethe Collection. Cf. Michaelis, *Jahrbuch*, XII, 1897, pp. 49-54; Reinach, *Répertoire de Statuaire*, II, p. 561, no. 2; Wace, *B. S. A.*, X, 1903-4, p. 107, D. 10.

Standing figure who has turned around as far as possible, and is making a gesture of thumb between fingers. He wears a cap on his curly hair and is slightly bearded. His hair in conventional rows of flat curls, suggests the Ethiopian. Ht. 0.145 m.

There is only one instance of a bronze Ethiopian life-size which, if it is genuinely an ancient work of sculpture, probably belongs in this period. Only the illustration in Reinach's Répertoire is available, and this shows the general appearance of the boy to be unlike all other classical representations of Ethiopians.

222. Tarragona. Cf. Reinach, *Répertoire de Statuaire*, IV, p. 353, no. 6.

Ethiopian boy, standing, with arms extended in front of him and palms upturned. His face is round and his build heavy. His hair is short and curly, his nose broad and his lips thick. His neck is awkward, being short and fat. The general appearance is unlike other ancient negroes.

In the Rhode Island School of Design in Providence is an unpublished interesting bronze head of a negro said to come from Alexandria.

CHAPTER IX

NEW HELLENISTIC EXPERIMENTS

Marble and Basalt

Previous to the Hellenistic era figurines were nearly all of the traditional terra-cotta with possibily a few of bronze, but in this period there was some experimenting in other materials. The suitability of some material inherently black for representing black skin now occurred to the sculptors and there are instances of basalt, black stone and black marble. One might expect a more frequent use of black materials, were it not that bronze itself suggests the negro skin so admirably and terra-cotta is so easily treated with black paint. However, the use of a black medium leaves no possible doubt as to the intention of the artist. Examples of black substance are as follows:

223. Athens—Polytechnikon—Demetriou Collection—from Alexandria. Cf. Puchstein, *Ath. Mitth.*, VII, 1882, pp. 15 and 16; Schreiber, *Ath. Mitth.*, X, 1885, p. 383 ff., pl. XII (wrongly called bronze); Reinach, *Répertoire de Statuaire*, II, p. 561, no. 6.

Basalt statuette of an Ethiopian boy, the arms broken off at the wrists and the legs broken off above the knees.

The hair is in close spiral curls all over the head, the nose broad and the lips thick and slightly parted, with the lower one protruding strongly. The hollow eye sockets were originally filled with some substance, probably silver, which has fallen away. There is a marked emphasis of the lower part of the facial structure. The whole is a very excellent and pleasing portrayal of the type.

The head inclines toward the right and the position of the arms shows that they were supporting some object on the left shoulder. The similar pose of the famous Châlon-sur-Saône statuette in the Bibliothèque Nationale, where the arms are placed as if holding the *trigonon,* or three-cornered lyre,

102 THE NEGRO IN GREEK AND ROMAN CIVILIZATION

indicates that the correct restoration would be with the lyre.
It is more prosaic but possible that he may be holding up a
platter in the fashion of a terra-cotta figure found at Myrina,
but the first interpretation seems more in keeping with the
expression of his face. Height 0.40 m.

224. Athens. Cf. Sybel, *Katalog der Skulpturen zu Athen*, no. 3110;
Schneider, *Jb. Kunst. Samml.*, III, 1885, p. 7, n. 6.

Head of an Ethiopian, of black stone.

225. Berlin, Königliche Museen, no. 493. Cf. Reinach, *Répertoire de
Statuaire*, II, p. 563, no. 8; Kekulé von Stradonitz, *Beschreibung der Skulpturen*, p. 192.

Black marble statuette of an Ethiopian who has sunk to
the ground and is resting on one knee. The awkwardness of
the pose is perhaps due to the restoration, as base, plinth, and
both legs below the knees are modern. His head turns toward
the left, and his hands are behind his back as if tied. His
hair is in long, conventionalized curls. His race is evidenced
by his hair, lips, and the dark material of which he is made.
Height 0.90 m. Also in Berlin (1579) is a black basalt head
of a negro boy from Asia Minor dating from the second century A. D. In the British Museum is a portrait of a young
Egyptian with curly hair, in green slate, from Alexandria,
second century B. C.

226. Newby Hall, Yorkshire—Vyner Collection. Cf. Michaelis,
Ancient Marbles in Great Britain, p. 534, no. 43; Schneider,
Jb. Kunst. Samml., III, 1885, p. 7, n. 6.

Bust of an Ethiopian of basalt (in the collection of Lady
Mary Vyner which was made by William Weddell, Esq.,
about the year 1765).

The experimenting artists of the Hellenistic era also attempted to show black in white. To represent an Ethiopian
in white marble called for no little skill, as the artist was
unaided in obtaining his effect by the color of his medium.
It was necessary to convey his meaning by telling delineation
of the physical marks of race. It is not surprising that such
use of marble was infrequent and in this period it is confined
to one example of relief sculpture, one statue in the round

in life size, two statuettes of great interest, and a remarkable gray marble head of a negress in the Museo delle Terme in Rome (illustrated in *Arch. Anz.* XXVI, 1911, p. 169).

227. Naples—Museo Nazionale. Cf. Rüsch, *Guida del Museo Nazionale*, p. 570, no. 6693; Reinach, *Répertoire de Reliefs*, III, p. 94, no. 1; Calza, *J. R. S.*, V, 1915, p. 169.

Biga driven by an Ethiopian with a warrior walking in front of the horses. The negro, shown in profile, has curly hair, snub nose, thick lips, and wears a simple tunic drawn in at the waist. He leans forward over the horses, holding the reins in his left hand.

The meaning of the scene has not been explained, though Reinach suggests the Busiris myth. This is very unlikely, as there is no suggestion of Heracles in the warrior and no apparent point of contact with the story. Perhaps the Ethiopian is a charioteer about to enter a contest in the hippodrome. It seems more probable that the Ethiopian is Memnon's chariot driver, and that the warrior who precedes the horses is none other than the hero himself.

228. Rome—Vatican—Galleria dei Candelabri. Cf. Visconti, *Museo Pio-Clem.*, III, 35, pl. 2, p. 236; Braun, *Ruinen u. Museen Roms*, p. 506, n. 208; Clarac, *Museé de Sculpture*, 883, 2250; Schneider, *Jb. Kunst. Samml.*, III, 1885, p. 6; Helbig, *Führer*, 3rd ed., I, p. 242, no. 375.

Pentelic marble statue of an Ethiopian slave boy, who carries in his left hand a ring from which are suspended a *strigil* and an ointment vessel for his master. His equipment shows him to be a bath attendant. The following are modern restorations: the right arm, shoulder and breast; the left side of the neck; part of the foot; and almost the whole support and plinth. The right hand has been restored as held out in front of him, holding a sponge. This is not an unlikely conjecture, for slaves holding sponges occur on the Corneto gem and a British Museum bronze. Helbig would prefer to have the hand restored as making some gesture to correspond with the mischief in the eyes, but this seems pointless.

One might expect some difference in the treatment of the

104 THE NEGRO IN GREEK AND ROMAN CIVILIZATION

negro features, some idealizing in this portrait on a larger
scale than the usual figurine, but this is not the case. The
hair is short and woolly, and the nose and mouth are characteristic, though by no means displeasing in effect. He is
probably a favorite attendant of some gentleman of the time,
who wished to have him immortalized in marble.

229. London—British Museum—Townsley Coll.—from Rome. Cf.
Clarac, V, pl. 825, 2223 a; Smith, *Catalogue of Greek Sculp-*
ture, III, p. 114, 1768; Schneider, *Jb. Kunst. Samml.*, III,
1885, p. 9; Collignon-Baumgarten, *Gr. Skulptur*, II, p. 616,
fig. 293; Wace, *B.S.A.*, X, 1903-4, p. 104, A. 8; Schreiber,
Ath. Mitth., X, 1885, p. 395.

Parian marble statuette of an Ethiopian acrobat balancing himself on his hands and chest with feet in the air
on the back of a crocodile. Head and neck are stretched forward. His hair is in corkscrew curls and his nose is short
and flat. The lips have been damaged so that their original
outline is not clear.

The statuette as shown in the Collignon illustration was
restored in certain parts, which have subsequently been removed. These are, according to Smith, the head and tail of
the crocodile, the right leg, left knee, the feet, and both elbows
of the acrobat, the forepaws and part of the rock plinth.
According to Clarac, the hands also are modern. Height 2 ft.
5¼ in., as restored.

230. Rome—Villa Patrizi. Cf. *Not. Scav.*, 1908, pp. 439 and 440;
Reinach, *Répertoire de Statuaire*, IV, p. 350, no. 1.

Marble statuette in the identical pose of the above, except
that there is a plain base instead of a crocodile and that the
hands are closed instead of being spread out on the base. The
legs are broken off at the knees, and very little of the base
remains. The notice of its excavation states that it was a
figure for a fountain.

The similarity of these two figures seems nowhere to have
been pointed out. The pose is identical and either one is a
copy of the other or both are copies of the same original.
The London statuette is poorer work, and its face lacks
entirely the liveliness of the other.

NEW HELLENISTIC EXPERIMENTS

The position of the two bodies is identical and the modelling of the flesh very similar, the differences consisting in the head, the base, and (if the London figure has been restored in that place) the hands. There is no evidence in the case of the Villa Patrizi figure that he is balancing on a crocodile. The treatment of the hair is far better in the latter statuette, the ringlets of curly hair being carefully modelled. The Ethiopian has a mischievous grin and both rows of teeth are indicated. The provenance of both is Rome, the former having been taken from Rome to London by the first Earl Cawdor, the other having been excavated in 1908 in the Via Nomentana. But the workmanship and the presence of the crocodile presuppose an Alexandrian original, if the figures are not themselves Alexandrian. Both figures are fountain figures.

It seems possible to connect the Villa Patrizi figure with another piece of sculpture, something which cannot often be done in the case of representations of Ethiopians in art. This is another fountain figure, a young satyr, which recently came into the Smith College Museum and is published in the Bulletin of Smith College, Hillyer Art Gallery, for May, 1920. There is also a replica of the satyr fountain figure in Copenhagen in the Glyptotek Ny Carlsberg. In Rome in the Museo Nazionale Romano [1] is also a statuette of a negro acrobat used as ornament of a fountain.

A comparison of the Villa Patrizi and Smith College figures reveals a similarity of treatment that leaves little doubt that the same sculptor modelled both. The outline of the form, the surface of the flesh and the delicate revelation of muscle show marked similarities. One common feature of both poses, though the satyr stands upright and the Ethiopian balances with feet in the air, is the sharp twist of the shoulder away from the chest necessitated by the supporting of a heavy weight. But the strongest resemblance is in the expression.

---

[1] Cf. Moretti, *I Monumenti d'Italia*, No. 20: *Il Museo Nazionale Romano*, p. 12, no. 29.

106 THE NEGRO IN GREEK AND ROMAN CIVILIZATION

Both figures have their lips parted in the same impish smile. Both are surely the work of the same hand, which probably specialized in fountain figures. It is significant that the head of a satyr was found with the Villa Patrizi figure.

Not the least interesting use of the Ethiopian head during this period was its adornment of necklaces and earrings. In fact, it is from its occurrence as a pendant or amulet in this and earlier periods that the theory has been deduced that the Ethiopian was considered prophylactic in antiquity. There is no statement to this effect in ancient literature.

There is great charm in a few necklaces, of which neck and loop of the clasp are soldered each to the top of a tiny Ethiopian head, carved in garnet, and held in place in the chain by a collar of gold filigree work. In spite of the small size of these heads every feature is clearly distinguishable. The goldsmiths of the Hellenistic period showed great skill in rendering the hair by tiny twisted spirals of fine gold wire affixed to the head in rows to represent curls.

Of the type of necklace with the Ethiopian's heads at the clasp, the following examples are known:

231. Dresden Museum. Cf. *Arch. Anzeiger*, VII, 1892, p. 168, fig. 38.
Necklace of roller-shaped beads of gold and carnelian, strung alternately. At each end it terminates in the head of an Ethiopian, carved from carnelian, and held in place by a collar of spiral gold and a wig of gold wire twisted into rings to indicate curls. The necklace fastens by means of a gold hook attached to one head and a gold loop for it to pass through, attached to the other.

232. London—British Museum—Burgon Collection—from a tomb on the island of Melos. Cf. Marshall, *Catalogue of Jewellery*, p. 216, no. 1961, pl. XXXVI.
Part of a necklace terminating in the heads of a negro (Marshall) and a negress respectively, carved in garnet, to which hook and loop are soldered in the manner described above. The hair is rendered by rows of spirals of gold wire,

NEW HELLENISTIC EXPERIMENTS 107

and the features are almost ape-like from the effect of the protruding lower jaw. From the evidence of the hair-dressing and the features, I consider that both heads represent women. The eyes were originally filled with some substance which has fallen away. Marshall places the work in the third century B. C.

233. London—British Museum—Franks Bequest. Cf. Marshall, *Catalogue of Jewellery*, p. 216, no. 1962, pl. XXXVI.

Necklace terminating at each end in the head of an Ethiopian woman, carved in garnet, the hair indicated by spiral coils of gold wire in rows. The lower part of the face is prominent. Work of the third century B. C.

234. London—British Museum—Franks Bequest. Cf. Marshall, *Catalogue of Jewellery*, p. 217, no. 1963.

Broken necklace, the end which is preserved terminating in the head of an Ethiopian woman carved in garnet, the hair rendered by coils of fine gold wire. Work of the third century B. C.

Of similar technique and closely resembling the heads on necklaces is an ear-ring from the same period:

235. London—British Museum—from a tomb at Cyme in Aeolis. Cf. Marshall, *Catalogue of Jewellery*, p. 186, no. 1709, pl. XXXI.

Ear-ring of twisted gold wire terminating in the head of an Ethiopian woman carved from garnet. Collar and hair are formed from coils of fine gold wire. The features are clear, and the profile is almost ape-like, with the protruding lower lip and jaw. Third century B. C. Height 0.019 m. Weight 30 grns.

The Ethiopian head as a pendant on a necklace, already met in the small objects from Naucratis and Cyprus, recurs again in the Hellenistic era on jewelry found in Italy and South Russia. The popularity of the type in Russia seems greater in this period than any other, as evidenced by the vases and terra cottas as well as the jewelry.

236. London—British Museum—found near Monteleone, Italy. Cf. Francica, *Oggetti d'Arte Greca*, pl. III; Marshall, *Catalogue of Jewellery*, p. 241, nos. 2114-6, pl. XLI.

108   THE NEGRO IN GREEK AND ROMAN CIVILIZATION

Three female heads of hollow gold, the thick lips showing
Ethiopian blood.   They have collars ornamented with gold
filigree work, and ear-rings in the form of great loops of gold
wire, which stand out at right angles to the head.   While
Marshall considers that they are either pin-heads or pendants,
it seems more likely that they are the latter, and that they
were held in place in the necklace by means of these loops.
Unless the ear-rings had some such function, it hardly seems
likely that they would be of such an exaggerated size.   Work
of the third century B. C.   Height 0.02 m.

237. London—British Museum—from Monteleone, Italy.   Cf. Francica, *Oggetti d'Arte Greca*, pl. III; Marshall, *Catalogue of
Jewellery*, p. 241, no. 2117, pl. XLI.

Pendant of hollow gold, with two heads in janiform fashion, both Ethiopian.   On either side is an ear-ring common to
both, and at the top is a wire loop by which it was suspended.
The noses are short and broad, and the lips thick.   Work of
the third century B. C.   Height 0.026 m.

238. Leningrad—Hermitage.   Cf. *Compte Rendu*, 1866, p. 74; Reinach, *Antiquités du Bosphore Cimmerien*, 2nd ed., p. 83,
pl. 32, no. 6.

Small Ethiopian masks, of gold, which served as pendants
on a necklace.   Found in graves in South Russia.

239. Leningrad—Hermitage.   Cf. Stephani, *Compte Rendu*, 1866,
p. 74; Reinach, *Antiquités du Bosphore Cimmerien*, 2nd ed.,
p. 83, n. 1.

Three Ethiopian's heads of dark blue glass, and one of
paste, which probably served as pendants on a necklace.

To this series of jewelry belongs also an example from
South Russia of an Ethiopian head as the head of a pin.

240. Leningrad—Hermitage.   Cf. Stephani, *Compte Rendu*, 1866,
p. 74; Duruy, *Histoire des Grecs*, vol. II, p. 170; Reinach,
Antiquités du Bosphore Cimmerien, 2nd ed., p. 54, pl. 12 a, 14.

Gold pin decorated with a negro head carved from sardonyx.

The Ethiopian head on gems seems to have passed out of
fashion, though a garnet carved with the design of an Ethi-

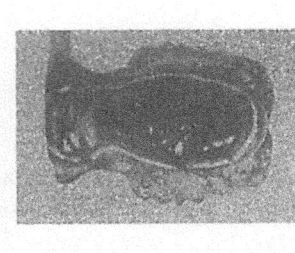

FIGURE 21.
AN AGATE FROM ALEXANDRIA.
In Collection of D. M. Robinson.

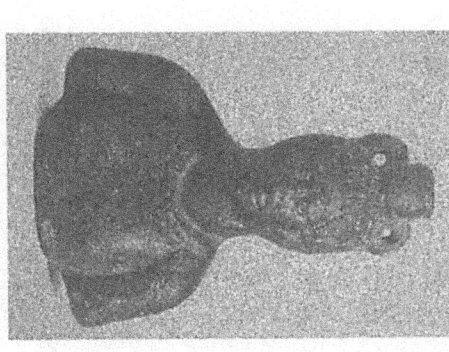

FIGURE 22.
CLAY VASE.
In Collection of D. M. Robinson.

FIGURE 23.
BRONZE ETHIOPIAN SLAVE CLEANING A BOOT
In the British Museum.

NEW HELLENISTIC EXPERIMENTS   109

opian mask may belong in this period, since garnet heads
appear on the necklaces and negro masks serve as pendants.

241. London—British Museum—Castellani Collection.   Cf. Smith,
   Engraved Gems, p. 188, no. 1767.

Garnet carved in cameo with the design of a negro mask
in front view.

242. Baltimore Collection of Professor D. M. Robinson—formerly in
   Collection of Charles T. Seltman.   Cf. *A. J. A.,* XXIV, 1920,
   pp. 18-26.

An interesting example of Greek work from Alexandria,
which Seltman believes to be connected with the ruling
family of Meroë and perhaps portrays them, is an agate carved
to represent three conjoined heads.   Part of the stone is black
and this has been carved with the features of an Ethiopian
woman.   The artist has shown geat skill in adapting a white
band in the stone so that it appears to be the edge of her veil.
The other two heads in lighter stone are a bearded man and
a youth with Ethiopian features.   Seltman suggests that this
is either the handle of the lid of a casket or the head of a
small sceptre, since a small vertical shaft has been drilled in
the center of the stone.   Height 1.25 m.   Fig. 21.

The conception and the style are unique in the history of
the Ethiopian type in art.   This tricephalic agate appears to
be genuine, and may serve to establish the authenticity of the
following gem in the British Museum now listed as doubtful,
since the subject is evidently the same:

243. London—British Museum—Castellani Collection.   Cf. C. Smith,
   Engraved Gems, p. 181, no. 1663.

Agate cut in cameo with the head of a veiled negress in
full front.   Authenticity doubtful.

The device of using the black part of the stone evidently
anticipates the process described by King to fit the design, in
connection with Renaissance cameos dating a little later than
1500 A. D.   He stated that this age was " extremely fruitful
in heads of negroes and also of negresses, the latter often in
the character of Cleopatra holding to her breast the asp.

110 THE NEGRO IN GREEK AND ROMAN CIVILIZATION

There is reason to believe that some of the latter are intended to commemorate the renowned black concubine of Clement VII, the mother of Alessandra dei Medici. Another reason, besides the celebrity of the sable beauty, that prompted the Florentine school to produce such swarms of miniature Ethiopians, was their discovery of the secret of staining black one of the layers of the common agate-onyx and obtaining thus the contrast, so great a desideratum in this style." Cf. C. W. King, *Antique Gems and Rings*, p. 326.

CHAPTER X

THE CHARACTER OF THE ETHIOPIAN

It is from the Hellenistic figurines that we can draw our clearest picture of Ethiopian slave life in the Greek world, depicted with a realism which the most accurate literary account could not match. Mythology is forgotten, the legendary Ethiopian of Homer has disappeared in an age of skepticism. There is no illusion about his origin, and therefore no mystery about his features. While his features were never idealized, they were in the fifth century invested with a certain charm. His features are now a study in ethnography, an exercise in skill at delineating odd type. The Ethiopian is a vogue, a fashion and a subject to be seized and made to pose as he goes about his daily work. The artists have caught him in varied attitudes and occupations; but all seem to have in common that they are not menial. The Ethiopian slave is sufficiently rare and fashionable so that he is reserved for personal service or for entertainment.[1] Not until there was no longer a scarcity of Ethiopians were they assigned to heavier and more degrading tasks. Their Greek masters evidently appreciated what are now considered to be among the best of the negro qualities—personal loyalty, ready laughter and a gift for song and dance. Boys were the favorite slaves with Ethiopian women apparently second in favor. The little slave boys, a vogue with the rich, run about waiting on their masters, carrying dishes and amphoras, filling vases for the banquet from wine skins. In the Ashmolean Museum is a terra-cotta negro boy (no. 197) from Tarentum, asleep beside an amphora, and an ascus in the form of a negro boy

---

[1] There is no doubt that they were slaves. A lecythus (G. 168) in the British Museum of Italic fabric of about 200 B. C. is in the form of an Ethiopian with hands crossed over his knees. On his breast is a placard showing that he is exposed for sale.

111

112 THE NEGRO IN GREEK AND ROMAN CIVILIZATION

bent over to the ground (1922. 205; from Thebes, third
century B. C.). In the British Museum Life room is a bronze
negro slave cleaning a boot, illustrated in *Guide to the Exhibition Illustrating Greek and Roman Life*, 1920, fig. 142 (no.
266, Fig. 23). A small bronze statuette of Hellenistic times
from Perugia acquired for the British Museum in 1908 shows
a negro slave with curly hair with his right hand on his hip
but his left hand raised high as if it originally carried a lamp.
If entertainment is required as well as butler service, they
sing songs which, to judge from the plaintive expression of
their faces, were the ancestors of the present-day negro
spirituals, and perhaps accompany themselves on the trigonon
(nos. 214, 223) in lieu of a banjo. If a more exciting offering is required, they dance a furious, barbaric dance, a tribal
dance of Africa, or perhaps a gentler measure more adapted
to Greek restraint (nos. 211, 212, Fig. 18). Perhaps they hold
boxing matches (no. 170) or even give an acrobatic perform-
ance with a tame crocodile (no. 229). And when their part of
the entertaining is over, they drop off to sleep in the usual
hunched-up crouching attitude (nos. 202, 220). They still
accompany their masters to the palaestra (no. 228) and sometimes go on a hunting expedition with him to carry his equipment (no. 179). Perhaps they gain a meagre living by hawk-
ing fruit on the streets of Alexandria with a pet monkey to
attract trade (no. 203), and their acrobatic stunts may have
been street performances. Possibly they entertained travellers
by diving for coins, a common sight in modern harbors (no.
209).

The only hint of education is the Ethiopian seated on a
rock, writing on a scroll (no. 169). Was he some special
slave, sufficiently valued by his owner so that it was considered worth while to train his intelligence?

It is in these figurines also that we first find in Greek art
any sense of the pathos of the Ethiopian's lot, though com-
passion for the life of a slave is found in Greek tragedies.
Heretofore the only emotional element present has been that

THE CHARACTER OF THE ETHIOPIAN   113

of humor and caricature; but among these terra-cottas and bronzes are a few which seem to show a consciousness of another mood. The artists regarded for an instant, not the strangeness which made the Ethiopian an object of entertainment to them, but the pathos of an exile from his own land (nos. 158, 159). This sentimentality is very fleeting and is nowhere met in the later and more matter-of-fact Roman art.

The distinction between a naturalistic representation and caricature is hard to make without having seen the original. This is no doubt the reason that in many museum catalogues heads and statuettes of Ethiopians are often wrongly called grotesques. From this the impression seems to have grown that the greater number of all ancient negro representations are grotesques, and their popularity has been explained from this standpoint. In reality we find among these figurines of Ethiopians very few of the distorted bodies and hideous faces which make the Alexandrian grotesques so distasteful, nearly all of them being simply cases of extreme naturalism. The few actual grotesques, and some of the realistic figurines, may perhaps be accounted for by the theory which Miss Richter advances, namely, that the grotesques represented stock characters in the mimes which had such an enormous popularity throughout the Hellenistic and Roman eras, and about the nature of which we have such scanty knowledge.

Euripides wrote a satyr play on the Busiris story in which he probably brought Ethiopians upon the stage, and both the Busiris and Andromeda myths were subsequently used by comedy writers. From the evidence of the vases, which often have comedy scenes and which frequently introduce Ethiopians, it is reasonable to suppose that the type became a familiar one on the comic stage. Certainly the evidence is circuitous and not direct, but it would be entirely natural that a race familiar in comedy and treated in caricature in art should develop into a stock character in the mime, perhaps the *Aithiops*. This would account for the masks of Ethi-

114 THE NEGRO IN GREEK AND ROMAN CIVILIZATION

opians used as pendants on necklaces, and particularly for the life-sized mask of terra-cotta which was evidently intended to be worn in some play, procession or ritual, since eyes, nose and mouth are pierced through, and there are holes above the ears for the cord which held it in place. An Ethiopian girl is introduced upon the stage in the Eunuchus of Terence which had a Greek comedy original. She has no part in the plot but undoubtedly added to the humor. If the *Aithiops* was actually a stock buffoon in comedies or mimes, the number of figurines and gems which show him crouching down on the ground and peacefully sleeping may mean that this characteristic inactivity was the laugh-producing rôle by which he entertained Greek audiences.

CHAPTER XI

THE ETHIOPIAN IN ROMAN LITERATURE

However great the variations between the objects which display the Ethiopian type in the different periods of Greek art, all had one feature in common. Whether they were jewelry for the adornment of the person or statuettes to ornament the house, the motif may be said to occur almost entirely on objects intended solely for decoration. The only exceptions to this classification are the vases, some of which were undoubtedly used though they are at the same time highly decorative.

The Roman usage, on the other hand, is as generally utilitarian as the Greek is decorative, and the type is principally found on objects which have a definite useful function in addition to their attractive appearance. An artistic usage so markedly different in two nationalities presupposes not only a different artistic spirit but a difference of attitude toward the race portrayed.

The paucity of references to actual (not mythical) Ethiopians in Greek literature and the spirit in which they are shown in Attic art make it safe to believe that in Greece proper, negroes in the flesh were comparatively rare, until the Alexandrian period at least, and that the impression they made was due to their rarity and unusual appearance. In the Hellenistic era their popularity is due to the opportunities which their physiognomy gave for the expression of the extreme naturalism of the day, and does not necessarily show that great numbers of them were at large in the Greek world. The evidence of Theophrastus (cf. p. 10) would indicate the contrary. The first Ethiopians filtered into the Greek world by way of the Greek colonies in Africa or were brought there by the Persian invasion, and we have no evidence that the Greeks imported any black slaves through military aggression.

115

The Romans on the other hand built up important colonies in Africa. The period of their establishment involved many military campaigns, and they were subsequently held by military rule. There can be no doubt that African tribes furnished the Romans with vast numbers of slaves and that in the Empire the dark races were a vastly more common sight at Rome than at Athens. The Romans would naturally be far more familiar with the Moor or Berber type of the Mediterranean colonies than with the South African. A more extensive knowledge of the latter races doubtless came when Rome took over the control of Egypt, where the type had been established for centuries. In this respect Roman literature gives scarcely more help than Greek in adding to our knowledge of the status of the Ethiopian at Rome. A study of the few references throws some light on the nomenclature employed to designate the dark-skinned races of the Roman world.

The earliest mention of Ethiopians occurs in the "Eunuchus" of Terence, where Parmeno has brought Thais what he considers two valuable gifts, a eunuch and an Ethiopian girl, and he complains of her indifference to his presents.

Nonne ubi mi dixti cupere te ex Aethiopia ancillulam, relictis rebus omnibus, quaesivi" ? II. 165-7.

This is obviously a Greek and not a Roman scene and reflects the Greek attitude already mentioned that an Ethiopian was an exceedingly choice slave to possess. The entrance of the Ethiopian girl must have been a great novelty upon the Roman stage at this time and probably produced an incidental bit of hilarious comedy which delighted Roman audiences. The features were probably exaggerated and the whole appearance of the girl made as comic as possible. Probably she was the counterpart of the slave woman owned by the impoverished farmer Linyius, described in the pseudo-Vergilian Moretum (ll. 31 ff.) :

erat unica custos
Afra genus, tota patriam testante figura
torta comam, labroque tumens et fusca colore
pectore lata, iacens mammis, compressior alvo,
cruribus exilis, spatiosa prodiga planta.

This poem also is not Roman but is generally felt to be a translation of a Greek original, probably Alexandrian. Its minute realism is surely in the spirit of the Alexandrian art which produced the negro figurines.

A certain vogue at Rome for Ethiopian attendants probably in imitation of the Greek custom is implied. The bath slave so frequently met in Greek art is recalled in the Auctor ad Herennium, IV, 50, 63 " ab avunculo rogetur Aethiops qui ad balneas veniat." That dark slaves were choice is shown by the fact that the Nemesis of Tibullus, II, 3, 55 is surrounded by dark slaves from India and places exposed to the sun's fire, though Ethiopians are not specified by name:

illi aint comites fusci quos India torret,
solis et admotis inficit ignis equis.

To this passage Kirby Flower Smith gives the following note: " Colored attendants were a luxury specially affected by women like Nemesis largely because, as in England and France during the seventeenth and eighteenth centuries, they suggested the fortune and position of foreign potentates, nabobs etc." It is the foregoing Latin passages which Melville-White, author of "The Gladiators," probably had in mind when he describes the lady Valeria as attended by a negro boy who held her mirror (opening of Chapter II).

The influence of the Greek attitude in the earlier literary passages is proved by the fact that the Greek word *Aithiops* is transliterated into Latin and that the relationship between dark skin and the sun persists in the Roman mind. As in Greek it seems to be a generic term for any dark-skinned man without regard to the finer distinctions of origin as it is considered synonymous with Maurus.

Niger, the adjective from which are derived words used in

9

so many modern languages to designate the blacks, seems not to have been used substantively for this purpose in antiquity. As an adjective definitely connected with a dark-skinned race it occurs once in Juvenal, who refers to the bony hand of a black Moor (nigri manus ossea Mauri, V. 53), and a Moor is not a negro. As an adjective denoting complexion it appears in Martial's unpleasant epigram listing half-breed children where it undoubtedly means black-skinned, Duae sorores iela nigra et haec rufa VI 39, 18. It is unlikely that an Ethiopian is meant in Vergil's second eclogue II. 16-18:

quamvis ille niger, quamvis tu candidus esses
o formose puer, nimium ne crede colori:
alba ligustra cadunt, vaccinia nigra leguntur.

Conington considers that the passage simply means a swarthy complexion. The same meaning may attach to *fuscus* as used by Ovid to describe Andromeda (*Heroïdes* XV, 36-7)

candida si non sum, placuit Cepheia Perseo
Andromede, patriae fusca colore suae

as here *fuscus* is again contrasted with *candidus*. Andromeda though never dark in Greek art nevertheless was a princess of Ethiopia and from Roman literature went down in French literary tradition as black. In Tibullus, II, 3, 55 quoted above *fuscus* was used of the dark races of Asia. For the people of India is used also the word *decolor*: compare Ovid, *Tristia*, V, 324—et quascumque bibit decolor Indus aquas; *Metamorph.* 4, 21—decolor extremo qua tinguitur India Gange; Propertius, IV, 3, 10—tunsus et Eoa decolor Indus aqua. That it was not always reserved for the people of India is shown by Juvenal who makes it synonymous with *Aithiops*, additional proof of the loose usage of this latter term in antiquity—Esse Aethiopis fortasse pater mox decolor heres impleret tabulas, VI, 600. The similarity of coloring between the people of India and Mauretania is observed by Lucan, IV, 678—tum concolor Indo Mauro.
The more restricted name Maurus is not often used with

THE ETHIOPIAN IN ROMAN LITERATURE   119

reference to black slaves at Rome. Martial writes with unmistakable contempt of the woolly hair of a Moor, VI 39, Hic qui retorte crine Maurus incedit.

The Roman attitude toward the Ethiopian as expressed in scattered passages is far less kindly than the Greek. The usage in Terence and the Auctor ad Herennium which imply a vogue for Ethiopians is probably in imitation of Greek usage. How early the Roman attitude crystalized into racial feeling it is hard to say, and as those who express it are chiefly satirists one must be careful in drawing conclusions. Nevertheless in the absence of any expressed good will and in the face of references which have a superior or contemptuous tone it is evident that the Romans had no special affection for Ethiopians at Rome, however romantically they may have spoken of the races of distant India.

The earliest passage in which they are spoken of slightingly seems to be in Cicero—cum hoc homine an cum stipite Aethiope, Cicero, *De Sen.*, 6. The word does not occur in all the manuscripts and the Oxford and Teubner texts omit it entirely. In notes it is translated "blockhead" and the statement made that in antiquity the Ethiopians were synonymous with stupidity, a conclusion obviously drawn from the passage and the modern attitude toward them. Even if the word was actually used by Cicero, this passage alone is basis for such a theory. That it was thought dangerous or at least bad luck to meet them is reflected in Juvenal, V, 54-5, et cui per mediam nolis occurrere noctem, clivosae veheris dum per monumenta Latinae. Cf. also Florus, IV, 7, et in aciem prodeuntibus obvius Aethiops minis aperte ferale signum fuit.

The physical characteristics of the Ethiopian were put forward with brutal realism in the *Moretum*, which undoubtedly had its influence whether it was original or a translation. Juvenal illustrates clearly that they had gone out of favor at Rome when he relates how a black Moor is delegated to serve the poor guests, while a more choice Asiatic slave waits on the patron and host. It is true that " duo Aethiopes capil-

120 THE NEGRO IN GREEK AND ROMAN CIVILIZATION

lati" carried wine between two of the countless courses of
Trimalchio's feast (cf. p. 79). Trimalchio's main object was
to show off the extent and variety of his retinue though perhaps Petronius is giving an additional example of a provincial
who brings Ethiopians into his dining-room when they had
gone out of favor as table attendants at Rome.

At Carthage Ethiopians were more highly esteemed probably than at Rome, as two Latin epigrams praise the Egyptian
hunter Olympius, who had undoubtedly given many a per-
formance in the amphitheater. Cf. *Anthologia Latina*
(Riese) I, Nos. 353, 354:

> Nil tibi forma nocet nigro fuscata colore
>
> .   .   .   .
>
> Vivet fama tui post te longaeva decoris
> Atque tuum nomen semper Karthago loquetur.

Certainly Martial has only scorn for them in VI, 36 and
VII, 87 and Juvenal sums up the racial feeling in the words
derideat Aethiopem albus, II, 23.

The Elder Pliny deals at some length with Ethiopia itself
but mentions no Ethiopians at Rome. The Ethiopians of
Greek mythology and poetry, burned by the sun, are recalled
in Macrobius (*Somn. Scip.*, 2, 10, 11—Aethiopes . . . quos
vicinia solis usque ad speciem nigri coloris exurit.

The immoral relations with them implied in Martial, VI,
39 and Juvenal, VI, 559-600 recall certain passages in the
Arabian Nights and doubtless had some basis in fact, though
they are probably the exaggeration of isolated incidents into
an accusation against the times after the manner of all
satirists.

Nevertheless the evidence of literature would not lead one
to anticipate any idealizing of the type in Roman art, and a
study of the objects shows a complete disillusionment in regard to the Ethiopians. Excessive propinquity has banished
the last traces of mythical Ethiopia.

CHAPTER XII

THE ETHIOPIAN IN ROMAN ART

The use most commonly made of the Ethiopian head at
Rome was its adaptation to small lamps, both of bronze and
terra-cotta. In these the head rests in a horizontal position,
and the hole for the wick is either the open mouth of the
Ethiopian or a nozzle projecting from his mouth. The
following is a partial list of such lamps:

BRONZE

244. London—British Museum—Towneley Collection. Cf. Walters,
Catalogue of Lamps, p. 4, no. 17.

Lamp in the form of an Ethiopian's head, face up. The
hair is indicated as thick and closely curling by means of
incised rings in the metal with a dot in the center of each.
A nozzle with a trefoil termination projects from the
Ethiopian's open mouth. Ht. 4⅛ in.

245. London—British Museum—Payne-Knight Collection. Cf. Walters, *Catalogue of Bronzes*, p. 328, no. 2531; Walters, *Catalogue of Lamps*, p. 4, no. 18.

Head of an Ethiopian, face up, with thick, woolly hair, a
plait of which forms the handle, and which is modelled even
on the cover of the filling-hole at the top of the head. He
holds the long nozzle in his open mouth. Length 3⅝ in. Also
in the Parthian room of the British Museum are bronze lamps
of the Hellenistic period in the form of a negro's head with
open mouth.

246. Paris—Bibliothèque Nationale—Caylus Collection. Cf. Caylus,
Recueil, vol. V, p. 252, pl. XC, no. 2, Babelon-Blanchet, *Catalogue des Bronzes*, p. 444, no. 1020.

Lamp in the form of an Ethiopian's head, face up, the hair
quilled in rows. The face is unpleasantly elongated. A
curved piece projects from the mouth to form the spout, and
the hole for filling is in the hair above the forehead. The

122   THE NEGRO IN GREEK AND ROMAN CIVILIZATION

cover, on which the hair was probably modelled also, is
missing. The eyes are wide open. Length 0.105 m.

247. Paris—Bibliothèque Nationale—Collection de Luynes. Cf. *Gaz.
Arch.*, V, 1879, p. 209, (illustrated in life size); Babelon,
Le Cabinet des Antiques, pp. 153 and 172; Babelon-Blanchet,
Catalogue des Bronzes, p. 444, no. 1019.

Lamp in the form of an Ethiopian's head, face up, with
hair in long curls standing out irregularly from his head.
All the features are exaggerated—the wide open eyes, high
cheek bones, short, flat nose, and huge, gaping mouth. The
forehead is long and retreating, the cover for the filling-hole
forming the upper part of the forehead. This lamp is one of
the most realistic of the series, and the best from an artistic
point of view.

247a. Helbig, *Bullettino*, 1874, p. 84.

Half of a bronze lamp from Alexandria in the form of an
Ethiopian's head. According to Helbig it has the peculiarity
that this half can function independently of the other half.

It is impossible to give a complete list of the many bronze
lamps with negro heads. There are good examples from
Aquileia, several in Trieste (Alinari photograph 3207). Cf.
also Loeschcke, *Lampen aus Vindonissa*, p. 480 (292), n.
457.

CLAY

248. London—British Museum—from Naucratis. Cf. Walters, *Catalogue of Lamps*, p. 60, no. 411.

Lamp in the form of an Ethiopian's head, with the filling-
hole in the forehead. The nozzle is missing. The hair is
thick and curly, the eye-brows are raised and the teeth indicated. Work of the Roman Period according to Walters.
Length 2½ in.

249. London—British Museum—from Armento. Cf. Walters, *Catalogue of Lamps*, p. 60, no. 412.

Lamp in the form of an Ethiopian's head, face up. The
mouth of the Ethiopian forms the wick-hole, and the lower
lip and chin are modelled below it. The eyes are half closed

THE ETHIOPIAN IN ROMAN ART   123

and the cheek-bones prominent. The lamp is glazed black.
Height 2¼ in.

250. London—British Museum—Hamilton Collection. Cf. Walters,
   Catalogue of Lamps, p. 60, no. 414.

Lamp, glazed dark brown, the top in the form of an Ethiopian's head with grotesque features. The mouth is grinning widely, exposing the teeth, and the hair is closely curled.
Length 5¼ in.

251. London—British Museum—from Alexandria. Cf. Walters, *Cata-
   logue of Lamps, p. 60, no. 415.

Unglazed clay lamp in the form of an Ethiopian's head, with the spout below his chin. His hair is in three rows of thick curls, his eyes are wide open and his nose is short and broad. Underneath the base is inscribed. Length 3⅜ in.

252. London—British Museum—from Egypt. Cf. Walters, *Catalogue
   of Lamps, p. 60, no. 416, pl. XI.

Lamp with black glaze, in the shape of an Ethiopian's head, the nozzle projecting from the wide open mouth. The curly hair is indicated by rings raised in the clay, set close together.
The eyes are wide open, the nose broad and flat. The upper row of teeth is indicated. Height 4¼ in.

253. London—British Museum—Towneley Coll. Cf. Walters, *Cata-
   logue of Lamps, p. 148, no. 984.

Lamp with plain handle and nozzle, the circular space between them containing the design of the head of a boy or an Ethiopian. The lamp has a dull red glaze. Roman work of the second century A. D. Length 4 in., diam. 2¾ in.

254. New Haven—Yale University—Stoddard Coll. Cf. Baur, *Cata-
   logue, p. 290, no. 656.

Lamp in the form of an Ethiopian's head, the open mouth forming the nozzle. The clay is light brown, with a red glaze.
The hair is indicated by raised rings in the clay. Ht. 2¼ in.

255. New Haven—Yale University—Stoddard Coll.—from Tarentum.
   Cf. Baur, *Catalogue,* p. 291, no. 662.

Fragment of a lamp from Tarentum, showing the head of an Ethiopian in relief. The clay is light brown, with a glaze shading from red to dark brown. The lips are thick, the nose short and the hair indicated by raised dots.

256. Toronto—Royal Ontario Museum of Archaeology, Inv. no. G 207 —Found at Fayum.

Unpublished lamp in the form of an Ethiopian's head. The nozzle is formed by his open mouth and his teeth are shown. The nose is flat and broad at the nostrils. He has high cheekbones and a high forehead.

Purely Roman are the bronze vases in the form of figurines or heads of Ethiopians, which probably served as receptacles for perfumes:

257. Paris—Bibliothèque Nationale. Cf. Du Mersan, *Histoire du Cabinet des Medailles*, p. 62, no. 127; Babelon-Blanchet, *Catalogue des Bronzes*, p. 441, no. 1011.

Bronze vase in the form of a crouching Ethiopian, asleep, his head between his knees and his fists pressed against either cheek. His nose is flat, his mouth is open, and his hair is arranged in symmetrical, flat locks against his head. A circular opening at the top of his head seems to indicate that he served as a perfume vase. Ht. 0.08 m.

258. Paris—Bibliothèque Nationale. Cf. Babelon-Blanchet, *Catalogue des Bronzes*, p. 442, no. 1014.

Bronze vase in the form of a sleeping Ethiopian, draped in a mantle, seated upon some object which he seems to guard. His head is wreathed in a garland, in grotesque contrast to his squat nose, thick protruding lips and fast-closed eyes. He probably served as a perfume vase. Ht. 0.114 m.

259. Paris—Bibliothèque Nationale—Collection de Janze. Cf. Babelon, *Gaz. Arch.*, 1884, pp. 204-206; Babelon, *Le Cabinet des Antiques*, pp. 51-3, pl. XVI; Babelon-Blanchet, *Catalogue des Bronzes*, p. 443, no. 1018.

Bronze head of an Ethiopian in the form of a vase. Parts of rings for a handle still remain in the hair.

This is a striking portrait of a fine type of African. The hair is thick, and arranged in long rows of curls about his head, and the beard also is rolled into eight separate curls which hang from his cheeks. The eyes are wide open and

THE ETHIOPIAN IN ROMAN ART   125

alert in expression. The cheek-bones are prominent, the nose short and broad, the mouth large and slightly open. Yet in spite of the faithful rendering of racial detail, there is a certain power in the expression of the face. Ht. 0.158 m.

260. Paris—Bibliothèque Nationale—Collection de Janze. Cf. Babelon-Blanchet, *Catalogue des Bronzes*, p. 442, no. 1015.

Bronze vase, probably a receptacle for perfume, in the form of the bust of an Ethiopian slave. His head is turned to the right, and his eyes are closed as if asleep. His hair is in formal curls. Ht. 0.057 m.

261. Odessa Museum—from Akkerman (ancient Tyras). Cf. Stern, *Jh. Oest. Arch. Inst.*, VII, 1904, pp. 187-203; Seltman, *A. J. A.*, XXIV, 1920, p. 14.

Bronze vase in the form of a bust of a young girl. An elaborate handle passes through two rings at the top of her head. She is called a negress by Stern, but Seltman is correct in failing to see any negro characteristics in the physiognomy beyond a suggestion of thickness in the lips. The coiffure in three tiers of soft curls is an example of the elaborate hairdressing of the Roman empire, rather than the woolly hair of an Ethiopian.

Not unlike the figurines in the form of vases are two ink-wells of bronze:

262. Paris—Bibliothèque Nationale—Collection de Janze. Cf. Babelon-Blanchet, *Catalogue des Bronzes*, p. 441, no. 1012.

A receptacle in the form of an Ethiopian slave, crouching on a cone-shaped eminence, with an oval opening between his feet which indicates that he served as an *atramentarium*. Both his knees are drawn up; his face rests on the palm of his left hand, with his elbow supported on his left knee, while his right hand rests on his right knee. Some drapery, tied about his waist, falls down in back of him. His hair is in rows of long curls, and his features are coarse. The eyes are staring in expression and the mouth is half open. Ht. 0.088 m.

126   THE NEGRO IN GREEK AND ROMAN CIVILIZATION

263. Paris—Bibliothèque Nationale—Caylus Collection. Cf. Babelon-Blanchet, *Catalogue des Bronzes*, p. 441, no. 1013; Caylus, *Recueil*, vol. III, p. 212, pl. LIV, 4; Creuzer-Guigniaut, *Religions de l'Antiquité*, pl. CLI, no. 581.

Receptacle in the form of a negro slave crouching on an eminence, with both knees drawn up and chin resting between them. He clasps with both hands a goatskin sack, which he supports on his back. His hair is in regular rows of curls, his eyes staring, his nose flat and his large mouth partly open. At the left of his feet is the repository for ink, a small vase with a conical cover. Ht. 0.069 m.

Even more utilitarian than lamps, perfume vases and inkwells are the small bronze busts of Ethiopians used as weights on steel-yards. Some are solid. Others are hollow, perhaps as a device for adjustment of the weight by filling them with some substance.

264. Fouquet Collection—from Tell-Moqdam (Leontopolis), Egypt. Cf. Perdrizet, *Collection Fouquet*, p. 57, no. 94, pl. XXV.

Bust of an Ethiopian boy, his head coiffed with a four-petalled flower upside down, through the stem of which is pierced the hole for suspension. His hair is in short curls arranged in rows; his forehead is concave above the temples; his eyes were originally inset with some substance which has fallen away, probably silver; his nose is short; his lips thick and slightly parted. Ht. 0.085 m.

265. Leipzig—Städtische Museum—Theodor Graf Collection. Cf. Schreiber, *Arch. Anz.*, V, 1890, p. 157, no. 7.

Bust of a negro with a round face, his hair falling about his head in long spiral curls. His forehead is concave and heavily wrinkled; his eyes are inset with silver; his nose is short and broad; and his thick lips are parted to show the upper row of teeth. On either side, at the top of his head, is a ring through which passed the handle by which he was suspended. Ht. 0.145 m.

Schreiber calls it a vase and suggests that it was used as a weight by filling it. Perhaps it served as a perfume vase. Neck and head are hollow.

THE ETHIOPIAN IN ROMAN ART   127

265a. Vase in Tübingen in form of negro bust. Ht. 0.06 m. From
Egypt. Cf. Goessler in *Antike Plastik, Amelung zum sech-*
zigsten Geburtstag, p. 80, fig. 5, p. 86.

265b. Baltimore—Coll. of David M. Robinson. Bought in Cairo.

Clay bust of negro with chain about the front of his neck
only, perfectly preserved, covered with black glaze. The Hellenistic prototype was of metal. Sad, almost weeping expression. Flat nose, two wrinkles in forehead. Hair arranged
like the Egyptian royal wig, in rectangles behind as well as in
front. On either side of opening suspension hole. Ht.
0.11 m. W. 0.08 m. Fig. 22. A replica of that in Tübingen.
Cf. Pagenstecher, *Expedition E. v. Sieglin,* II, 3, p. 205, pl.
29; *Antike Plastik Amelung,* 1928, p. 80, fig. 6.

266. London—British Museum—Hertz Coll. Cf. *Arch. Zeit.,* 1843,
p. 203; *Hertz Coll. Sale Catalogue,* 1859, no. 587; Smith,
Guide Illustrating Greek and Roman Life, 1920, fig. 142;
Walters, *Catalogue of Bronzes,* p. 269, no. 1876, fig. 27;
Reinach, *Répertoire de Statuaire,* III, p. 158, no. 3.

Bronze figurine of an Ethiopian slave cleaning a boot
(*calceus*), crouching down and supporting himself on his
right knee. He holds the boot in his left hand and applies
the sponge to it with his right. His woolly hair, indicated
by rows of raised dots, is bound with a fillet. From the top
of his head rises a cylindrical eminence pierced through with
a hole. This was probably for a ring by means of which the
figure could be suspended. Ht. 4 in. Fig. 23.

267. London—British Museum—Castellani Collection. Cf. Walters,
Catalogue of Bronzes, p. 269, no. 1677

Bust of an Ethiopian, with a suspension ring at the back
of his neck. He wears a conical cap, and his eyes are inset
with garnets. Ht. 6 in.

268. Paris—Bibliothèque Nationale—Caylus Collection. Cf. Caylus,
Recueil, Vol. IV, p. 316, pl. XCVII, nos. 3 and 4; Babelon-
Blanchet, *Catalogue des Bronzes,* p. 446, no. 1025.

Bust of an Ethiopian set in a three-petalled flower which
covers part of his chest. The hair is in three rows of flat
curls, but the features are not negroid. Babelon and Blanchet
consider the bust a negro, but Caylus makes no mention of

128 THE NEGRO IN GREEK AND ROMAN CIVILIZATION

the possibility of negro blood and thinks it represents a
woman. The ring for suspension is at the top of the head.
Ht. 0.1 m.

269. Zurich—Sammlung der Universität. Cf. Blümner, *Führer*, p.
119, no. 2073.

Head of an Ethiopian, used as a weight, from lower Italy.

There is a group of four small bronze busts of Ethiopians,
the purpose of which is obscure. They represent the upper
part of divers, with arms stretched out in front and with a
flat metal extension at their backs. If they were uniform in
weight, their flat bases might mean that they were balance
weights. From their general shape they might have been
handles on the lid of some bronze receptacle.

270. Iena—Schott Collection. Cf. *Coll. Schott à Iena*, A 1475;
Reinach, *Répertoire de Statuaire*, III, p. 158, no. 6.

Head and arms of an Ethiopian, of bronze, with thick lips
and hair in spiral curls. He holds some objects (probably a
shell-fish) between his out-stretched hands. There is a short
metal extension from his back. The position of his head,
which is thrust back as if being held out of water, and the
object in his hands, show that he is a diver.

271. London—British Museum—Payne-Knight Collection. Cf.
Walters, *Catalogue of Bronzes*, p. 269, no. 1674.

Upper part of a diver with woolly hair and Ethiopian
features. His arms are extended in front of him and he holds
between his hands a shell-fish which he has just brought up.
At his back is a flat metal extension. Length 5¼ in.

272. London—British Museum. Cf. Walters, *Catalogue of Bronzes*,
p. 269, no. 1675.

Bronze bust of an Ethiopian diver similar to the foregoing,
but without the metal extension. The hair is more sym-
metrically arranged. Length, 4¾ in.; ht. 1¾ in.

273. Bibliothèque Nationale. Cf. Babelon-Blanchet, *Catalogue des
Bronzes*, p. 443, no. 1017.

Bronze bust of an Ethiopian diver, similar to the foregoing.

THE ETHIOPIAN IN ROMAN ART 129

He has the long metal extension at his back. Ht. 0.042 m.; length, 0.091 m.

The Bibliothèque Nationale has two bronze nails which terminate in the head of an Ethiopian:

274. Paris—Bibliothèque Nationale. Cf. Babelon-Blanchet, *Catalogue des Bronzes*, p. 445, no. 1023.

Bronze nail with the head of an Ethiopian in semi-round relief style, at the top. Roman work. Ht. 0.034 m.

275. Paris—Bibliothèque Nationale. Cf. Babelon-Blanchet, *Catalogue des Bronzes*, p. 445, no. 1024.

Bronze nail with head similar to the foregoing. Ht. 0.025 m.

There is a single instance of a bronze terminal figure with an Ethiopian's head, which probably marked the boundary of some Roman gentleman's property:

276. Oxford—Ashmolean Museum—Fortnum Collection. Cf. Michaelis, *Ancient Marbles in Great Britain*, p. 661, no. 18; Schneider, *Jb. Kunst. Samml.*, III, 1885, p. 7, n. 6.

This completes the list of adaptations of the motif to utilitarian objects. Most of them are commonplace, and only a few are of value from the artist's standpoint. More care has been expended in the workmanship of two bronze pendants, which seem to be the sole survivals of the Greek and Etruscan use of the type on jewelry, since a gold mask of the Roman period from Egypt is too large to be an ornament.

277. Paris—Bibliothèque Nationale. Cf. Babelon-Blanchet, *Catalogue des Bronzes*, p. 445, no. 1021.

Bronze pendant in the form of the head of an Ethiopian boy. His hair is in three rows of spiral curls, radiating from the top of his head, where the ring for suspension is fastened. His eyes are wide open, his nose snub, and his lips thick. On his neck is a collar ornamented with a *bulla*. Height 0.062 m.

278. Paris—Bibliothèque Nationale. Cf. Babelon-Blanchet, *Catalogue des Bronzes*, p. 445, no. 1022.

Circular bronze pendant, the border encrusted with silver.

130 THE NEGRO IN GREEK AND ROMAN CIVILIZATION

The center has an ornamentation, applied on it, the head of an Ethiopian modelled in bronze, in high relief. His hair is in spiral curls, his nose is snub and his lips are thick. The hole for suspension is in the border above the head. Diam. 0.04 m.

279. London—British Museum. Cf. Marshall, *Catalogue of Jewellery*, p. 369, no. 3094.

Gold mask of a negro, his hair indicated by raised dots. Work of the Roman period, from excavations at Benghazi and Teuchira. Ht. 0.14 m.

Among the purely decorative bronzes are two busts published by Bienkowski, in which a woman of Moorish type is used as a personification of Africa; coins of Mauretania and Numidia display a similar type.

280. Algiers—in a private collection—from Berroughia. Cf. *Rev. Arch.*, 1891, pp. 380-384; Bienkowski, *Corporis Barbarorum Prodromus*, p. 94.

Bronze bust similar to the foregoing but of poorer workmanship.

281. Constantine Museum—from Thibilis (Announa). Cf. Doublet-Gaukler, *Musée de Constantin*, pl. IX; Bienkowski, *op. cit.*, p. 94.

Bronze bust of a woman personifying Africa, with round flat face, full cheeks and thick lips. Her hair falls in three rows of spiral curls.

282. Coins of Mauretania and Numidia. Cf. L. Müller, *Monnaies de l'ancienne Afrique*, III, p. 43, no. 58; 100, 15, 107, 1; Bienkowski, *Corporis Barbarorum Prodromus*, p. 94.

Coins with the type of a female head personifying Africa, her hair in long spiral curls.

There remain to be described only a few decorative bronzes and marbles. Most of these are of as fine workmanship as any portraits of Ethiopians which Greece produced. They may be the work of Greek artists at Rome. The last of them, a marble head in life size, is from every standpoint the finest portrait of a man with Ethiopian blood. Fig. 24.

THE ETHIOPIAN IN ROMAN ART   131

283. Rome—Villa Albani—Galleria de Canopo. Cf. Brunn-Arndt-Bruckmann, *Griechische und Römische Porträts*, pls. 729-730; Helbig, Fuehrer³, II, p. 456, no. 1926.

Life-sized marble bust assigned to the Flavian period from the cutting of the hair, which is similar to that of female portraits of the period. The man is called a barbarian with negro blood. Before deciding as to his race, one must imagine away the restorations, which include: most of the nose; part of the ears; most of the bust and part of the panther skin which hangs over his shoulder. The nose has been restored as long and pointed, and there is no clue as to its original outlines. When the nose is covered over the effect of the face is more negroid. The hair is tightly curling all over the head, and the lips are fairly thick, although the mouth is not large. The panther skin would seem to point to an African origin.

284. Sousse—Tunis. Cf. *Musée de Sousse*, pl. 13; Reinach, *Répertoire de Statuaire*, III, p. 273, no. 5.

Black marble head and torso of an Ethiopian boy, who holds a pigeon in his left hand. His hair is short and thickly curling, his nose snub and his lips thick. His head bends toward the bird in his hand. The right arm below the elbow is missing, and the legs below the knee. The work is probably of the Roman period, since Susa was a Roman colony.

285. Fould Collection. Cf. Chabouillet, *Description des Antiquités de M. L. Fould*, no. 875; Schneider, *Jb. Kunst. Samml.*, III, 1885, p. 7, n. 6.

Head of an Ethiopian of serpentine marble. It is probably a work of the Roman period, because of the use of colored marble.

286. Baltimore—Walters Gallery—from Rome. Cf. *Mél. d'Arch. et Hist.*, 1888, pl. 12; Reinach, *Répertoire de Reliefs*, II, p. 196, no. 1.

In the "Triumph of Dionysus," principal relief on a marble sarcophagus from the burial ground of the Licinii Crassi on the Via Salaria, two Ethiopian children are shown riding each on the back of one of the two panthers who draw the triumphal car of the god.

132 THE NEGRO IN GREEK AND ROMAN CIVILIZATION

287. Ostia. Cf. Calza, *J. R. S.*, V, 1915, pp. 164-169; Ostia, *Historical Guide to the Monuments* (trans. by Weeden-Cooke), p. 189, fig. 53; A. de Ridder, *Revue des Études Grecques*, XXX, 1917, p. 199.

Small bronze bust of an Ethiopian boy wearing a tunic, a sleeved cloak, (*paenula*) and a hood (*cucullus*) which is drawn over his shoulder and held by his left hand. The hair is a mass of short curls, the nose snub, the lips thick and parted. The work is excellent in the rendering of detail. The individual and racial characteristics are rendered in a most lifelike manner, even to a bump on the forehead above the right eye. It was found in the house of a baker adjoining his bakeshop.

288. Paris—Bibliothèque Nationale. Cf. Babelon-Blanchet, *Catalogue des Bronzes*, p. 442, no. 1016.

Small bronze bust of an Ethiopian boy, his hair in curls, his lips thick, protruding and partly open. A strap is slung over his shoulder and hangs down his chest to the left, as if he were carrying some object suspended by it on that side. Ht. 0.045 m.

289. Berlin—Koenigliche Museen—from Thyreatis. Cf. Schrader, *Berlin Winckelmannspr.*, LX, 1900; *Jb. der Koenigl. Preuss. Kunstsamml.* XXI, 1900, p. 1; Hekler, *Bildniskunst*, p. 281; Kekulé von Stradonitz, *Griech. Skulptur*, p. 370; Brunn-Arndt-Bruckmann, folio 69, pls. 689-690; F. von Bissing, *Ath. Mitth.*, XXXIV, 1909, p. 31; *Bull. Ac. Danemark*, 1913, pp. 418 and 427; Dickins, *Hellenistic Sculpture*, p. 28; Graindor, *B. C. H.*, XXXIX, 1915, pp. 402-412.

Life-sized marble head of a man with unmistakable Ethiopian blood. His woolly hair, cut close to his head, is wonderfully rendered in the marble. He is markedly dolichocephalic and his forehead is low and retreating. The eyes are large, prominent and set wide apart, and the pupils are indicated by small round hollows in the surface. The nose is broken off, but enough remains to show that it must have been fairly short and broad at the nostrils. The lips are thick, though the mouth is not large. The hair of the growing beard is skilfully indicated on the cheeks, chin and upper lip. The ears are small and set low in the head below the line of the eyes. The marble has taken on a patina which creates the

FIGURE 24a.
MARBLE HEAD OF ETHIOPIAN.
In Berlin

Reproduced from Brunn-Arndt-Bruckmann, *Griechische und Römische Porträts*.

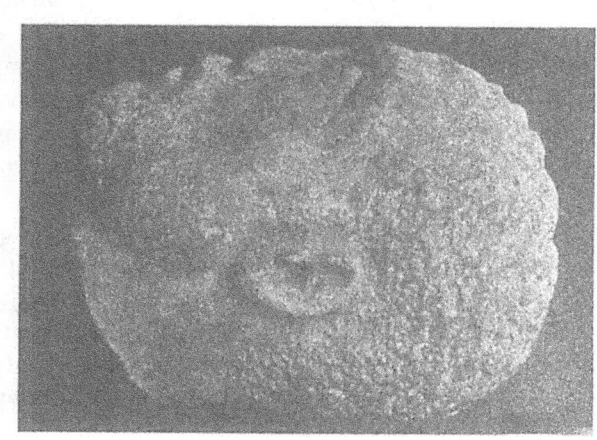

FIGURE 24b.
PROFILE OF FIGURE 24a.

THE ETHIOPIAN IN ROMAN ART 133

illusion of dark skin, though the marble was originally white. There is no prominence of the jaw structure and consequently no trace of savagery in the effect. The intelligent expression of the eyes offsets the low forehead.

Schrader in his original publication of the head concludes that the technique is that of the second or possibly third century A. D. This was a period of realism in portraiture and it is safe to assume that we have here a fair likeness which is reliable evidence in identifying him. Both the unusual facial type and the date assigned to the workmanship favor the theory offered by Graindor that this splendid work of art represents a certain Memnon, one of the three τρόφιμοι of Herodes Atticus, the famous patron of art and learning in the reign of the emperor Hadrian. The head was found at Thyreatis (near the modern Loukou) in the Peloponnesus, in land that has subsequently proved to be property once owned by Herodes Atticus. It is known from literature that Herodes set up herms of his *trophimi* after their deaths (Graindor, *loc. cit.*) and herms of the other two, with inscriptions, have been found on other estates. There is every reason to believe that the marble head now in Berlin once was part of a marble herm of the third τρόφιμος, Memnon, set up by Herodes Atticus on this Peloponnesian estate. There could be no better name for a man with Ethiopian blood than one associated with the most famous king of legendary Ethiopia. Likewise Schrader had concluded from the care given to every detail of hair and beard that the head belonged to a bust intended to be inspected at close range, rather than a full-sized statue set upon a pedestal.

The skill of the artist is revealed in the way in which he has contrived to unite in the face at the same time the marks of refinement and of primitive origin. The combination of Greek skill and Roman fidelity to nature make this head a fitting close for the long series of representations of the Ethiopian race in the art of the two great states of the ancient world. Figs. 24 a and b.

10

BIBLIOGRAPHY

Amelung, Walther, *Die Skulpturen des Vaticanischen Museums*. Berlin, 1908. 2 vols.

Babelon, Ernest, *Traité des monnaies grecques et romaines*. Paris, 1907.

———, and Blanchet, J. Adrien, *Catalogue des bronzes antiques de la Bibliothèque Nationale*. Paris, 1895.

Baumeister, A., *Denkmäler des klassischen Altertums*. Munich, 1885.

Baur, Paul V. C., *Catalogue of the Rebecca Darlington Stoddard Collection of Greek and Italian Vases in Yale University*. New Haven, 1922.

Beazley, J. D., *Attic Red-Figured Vases in American Museums*. Cambridge, 1918.

———, *The Lewes House Collection of Ancient Gems*. Oxford, 1920.

Benndorf, Otto, and Schöne, Richard, *Die antiken Bildwerke des Lateranensischen Museums*. Leipzig, 1867.

Bienkowski, Petrus, *De Simulacris Barbarorum Gentium apud Romanos—Corporis Barbarorum Prodromus*. Krakow, 1900.

Blanchard, Louis, *Le Trésor d'Auriole et les dieux nègres de la Grèce*. Marseilles, 1870.

Blümner, H., *Führer durch die archaeologische Sammlung der Universität Zürich*. Zurich, 1914.

Boehlau, Johannes, *Aus ionischen und italischen Nekropolen*. Leipzig, 1898.

Brandis, J., *Das Münz-und Gewichtswesen in Vorderasien*. Berlin, 1866.

Brunn, Henrich, *Geschichte der griechischen Künstler*. 2nd ed. Stuttgart, 1889.

Brunn—Bruckmann, *Griechische und römische Porträts*. Munich, 1904.

Bulle, Heinrich, *Der schöne Mensch im Altertum*. Munich, 1912.

Buschor, Ernst, translated by Richards, G. C., *Greek Vase Painting*. Oxford, 1921.

Carnegie, Lady Helena, *Catalogue of the Southesk Collection of Ancient Gems*. London, 1918.

Caskey, L. D., *Catalogue of Greek and Roman Sculpture*. Boston, Museum of Fine Arts, 1925.

Caylus, Comte de, *Recueil d'Antiquités égyptiennes, étrusques, grecques, romaines et gauloises*. Paris, 1759.

Clarac, Comte de, *Musée de Sculpture Antique et Moderne*. Paris, 1839.

135

Collignon, Maxime, Les Statues funéraires dans l'Art grec. Paris, 1911.

——, translated by Baumgarten, Fritz, Geschichte der griechischen Plastik. Strassburg, 1898.

Corey, Arthur D., De Amazonum Antiquissimis Figuris. (Diss.) Berlin, 1891.

Corpus Vasorum Antiquorum. Published by Union Académique Internationale. Paris.

Cultrera, G., Vasi Dipinti del Museo di Villa Giulia. Monumenti Antichi, XXIV, pp. 396-7.

Delbrück, Richard, Antike Porträts. Bonn, 1912.

Dickins, Guy, Hellenistic Sculpture. Oxford, 1920.

Dumont, Albert, and Chaplain, Jules, Les Céramiques de la Grèce propre. Paris, 1888.

Evans, Sir Arthur, The Palace of Minos. London, 1921. Two volumes have so far appeared.

Fairbanks, Arthur, Athenian Lekythoi with Outline Drawing of Glaze Varnish on a White Ground. New York, 1907. University of Michigan Studies, Humanistic Series, vol. VI.

——, Athenian Lekythoi with Outline Drawing in Matt Color on a White Ground. New York, 1914. University of Michigan Studies, Humanistic Series, vol. VII.

Fontenay, Eugène, Les Bijoux anciens et modernes. Paris, 1887.

Friederichs, Carl, and Wolters, Paul, Die Gipsabgüsse antiker Bildwerke—Königliche Museen zu Berlin. Berlin, 1885.

Froehner, Wilhelm, Collection Julien Gréau—Verrerie, Émaillerie et Poterie appartenant à M. John Pierpont Morgan. Paris, 1903.

——, Deux Peintures de Vases grecs de la Necropole de Cametros. Paris, 1871.

——, Terres Cuites d'Asie de la Collection Julien Gréau. Paris, 1886.

Furtwängler, Adolf, Aigina—Das Heiligtum der Aphaia. Munich, 1906.

——, Beschreibung der geschnittenen Steinen im Antiquarium—Königliche Museen zu Berlin. Berlin, 1896.

——, Beschreibung der Vasensammlung im Antiquarium—Königliche Museen zu Berlin. Berlin, 1885.

——, La Collection Sabouroff—Monuments de l'Art grec. Berlin, 1887.

Furtwängler und Reichhold, Griechische Vasenmalerei. Munich, 1904—.

Gardner, Ernest A., A Catalogue of the Greek Vases in the Fitzwilliam Museum, Cambridge. Cambridge, 1897.

BIBLIOGRAPHY

Gardner, Percy, *Catalogue of the Greek Vases in the Ashmolean Museum*, Oxford, 1893.

———, *The Types of Greek Coins*. Cambridge, 1883.

Grundy, G. B., *The Great Persian War and its Preliminaries*. London, 1901.

Gruppe, O., *Griechische Mythologie und Religionsgeschichte*. Munich, 1906.

Hadaczek, Karl, *Der Ohrschmuck der Griechen und Etrusker*. Vienna, 1903.

Hartwig, Paul, *Die griechischen Meisterschalen der Blüthezeit des strengen rothfigurigen Stiles*. Berlin, 1893.

Hekler, Anton, *Die Bildniskunst der Griechen und Römer*. Stuttgart, 1912.

Helbig, Wolfgang, *Führer durch die öffentlichen Sammlungen klassischer Altertümer in Rom*. Leipzig, 1912.

Herford, Mary A. B., *A Handbook of Greek Vase Painting*. Manchester, 1919.

Heuzey, Leon, *Les Figurines antiques de terre cuite du Musée du Louvre*. Paris, 1883.

Heydemann, Heinrich, *Die Vasensammlungen des Museo Nazionale zu Neapel*. Berlin, 1909.

Hoppin, Joseph Clark, *A Handbook of Greek Black-Figured Vases*. Paris, 1924.

———, *A Handbook of Attic Red-Figured Vases*. 2 vols. Paris, 1919.

Hoeber, Fritz, *Griechische Vasen*. Munich, 1909.

Kekulé von Stradonitz, Reinhard, *Bescholreibung der antiken Skulpturen—Königliche Museen zu Berlin*. Berlin, 1891.

———, *Die Terrakotten von Sicilien*. Berlin, 1884.

King, C. W., *Antique Gems and Rings*. London, 1872.

Klein, Wilhelm, *Geschichte der griechischen Kunst*. Leipzig, 1907.

———, *Die griechischen Vasen mit Lieblingsinschriften*. Leipzig, 1898.

Lippold, Georg, *Gemmen und Kameen des Altertums und der Neuzeit*. Stuttgart.

de Longpérier, Adrien, *Notice des antiquités assyriennes, babyloniennes, perses, hebraïques exposées dans les galeries du Musée du Louvre*. Paris, 1854.

J. Loewenherz, *Die Aethiopen der altclassischen Kunst*, Göttingen, 1861.

Lung, G. E., *Memnon. Archäologische Studien zur Aithiopis*. Bonn, 1912.

Marshall, F. H., *Catalogue of the Finger-Rings, Greek, Roman and Etruscan, in the British Museum*. London, 1907.

137

Marshall, F. H., *Catalogue of the Jewellery, Greek, Roman and Etruscan in the British Museum.* London, 1911.
Martha, Jules, *L'Art Etrusque.* Paris, 1889.
Masner, Karl, *Die Sammlung antiker Vasen und Terrakotten im K. K. Oesterreich. Museum.* Vienna, 1892.
Michaelis, Adolf, translated by Fennell, C. M., *Ancient Marbles in Great Britain.* Cambridge, 1882.
Millingen, James, *Ancient Unedited Monuments. Painted Greek Vases, from Collections in Various Countries.* London, 1822.
Myres, John L., *Handbook of the Cesnola Collection of Antiquities from Cyprus.* New York, 1914.
Myres, John L., and Richter, Max O., *A Catalogue of the Cyprus Museum.* Oxford, 1899.
Müller, C. O., and Wieseler, Friedrich, *Denkmäler der alten Kunst.* Göttingen, 1854.
Nauck, Augustus, *Tragicorum Graecorum Fragmenta.* Leipzig, 1889.
Nicole, Georges, *Catalogue des Vases Peints du Musée National d'Athènes.* Paris, 1911.
Niessen, Carl Anton, *Beschreibung römischer Altertümer gesammelt von Carl Anton Niessen.* Cologne, 1911.
Ny Carlsberg Glyptotek, *Billedtavler til Kataloget over Antike Kunstvaerker.* Copenhagen, 1907.
Ohnefalsch-Richter, Max, *Kypros. The Bible and Homer.* London, 1893.
Osborne, Duffield, *Engraved Gems, Signets, Talismans and Ornamental Intaglios, Ancient and Modern.* New York, 1912.
Panofka, Theodore, *Antiques du Cabinet du Comte de Pourtalès-Gorgier.* Paris, 1834.
Pellegrini, Giuseppe, *Museo Civico di Bologna. Catalogo dei Vasi Greci Dipinti delle Necropoli Felsinee.* Bologna, 1912.
Perdrizet, Paul, *Bronzes grecs d'Égypte de la Collection Fouquet.* Paris, 1911.
Perrot, Georges and Chipiez, Charles, *Histoire de l'art dans l'antiquité.* Vol. X, 1914. Paris.
Pfuhl, Ernst, *Malerei und Zeichnung der Griechen.* 3 vols. Munich, 1923.
Pottier, Edmond, *Catalogue des Vases antiques de terre cuite. Musée National du Louvre. Troisième partie.* Paris, 1906.
———, *Les Statuettes de terre cuite dans l'antiquité.* Paris, 1890.
———, *Vases antiques du Louvre.* Paris, 1901.
Pottier, Edmond, and Reinach, Salomon, *La Necropole de Myrina.* Paris, 1887.
Preller, *Griechische Mythologie.* Berlin, 1872.
———, *Die griechische Heldensage.* Berlin, Carl Robert, 1921.

BIBLIOGRAPHY

Rayet, Olivier. *Monuments de l'art antique.* Paris, 1884.

Rayet, Olivier, and Collignon, Maxime, *Histoire de la céramique grecque.* Paris, 1888.

Reinach, Salomon, *Antiquités du Bosphore Cimmerien.* Paris, 1892.

——, *Répertoire de reliefs grecs et romains.* Paris, 1909.

——, *Répertoire de la statuaire grecque et romaine.* Paris, 1897.

——, *Répertoire des vases peints grecs et étrusques.* 2 vols. 1899-1900.

Richter, Giseła M. A., *The Craft of Athenian Pottery. An Investigation of the Technique of Black-Figured and Red-Figured Athenian Vases.* New York, 1923.

——, *Greek, Etruscan and Roman Bronzes in the Metropolitan Museum of Art.* New York, 1915.

de Ridder, A., *Catalogue des vases peints de la Bibliothèque Nationale.* Paris, 1902.

——, *Collection de Clercq. Les Terres Cuites et les verres.* Paris, 1909.

——, *Musée du Louvre. Les Bronzes antiques.* Paris, 1913.

Riezler, Walter, *Weissgrundige attische Lekythen.* Munich, 1914.

Robinson, Edward, *Museum of Fine Arts, Boston—Catalogue of Casts, Part III. Greek and Roman Sculpture.* Boston, 1900.

Roux Aîné, H., and Barré, M. L., *Herculaneum et Pompei—Recueil général des peintures, bronzes, mosaïques.* Paris, 1872.

Ruesch, A., *Guida del Museo Nazionale di Napoli.*

della Seta, Alessandro, *Museo di Villa Giulia.* Rome, 1918.

Schaal, Hans, *Griechische Vasen aus Frankfurter Sammlungen.* Frankfurt, 1923.

Scheurleer, C. W. L., *Catalogus eener verzameling egyptische grieksche romeinsche en andere Oudheden.* 's-Gravenhage, 1909.

Sieveking, J., *Die Terrakotten der Sammlung Loeb.* 2 vols. Munich, 1916.

Smith, A. H., *A Catalogue of Engraved Gems in the British Museum.* London, 1888.

——, *A Catalogue of Sculpture in the Department of Greek and Roman Antiquities, British Museum.* London, 1904.

——, *Marbles and Bronzes in the British Museum.* London, 1914.

Smith, Cecil, *A Guide to the Exhibition Illustrating Greek and Roman Life, British Museum.* London, 1920.

Studniczka, Franz, *Kyrene, eine altgriechische Göttin.* Leipzig, 1890.

Svoronos, *Das Athener National-Museum.* Athens.

Seltman, C. T., *Athens. Its History and Coinage before the Persian Invasion.* Cambridge, 1924.

189

Tillyard, E. M. W., *The Hope Vases—a Catalogue and a Discussion of the Hope Collection of Greek Vases with an Introduction on the History of the Collection and on Late Attic and South Italian Vases.* Cambridge, 1923.

Walters, H. B., *Catalogue of the Bronzes, Greek, Roman and Etruscan, in the Department of Greek and Roman Antiquities, British Museum.* London, 1899.

——, *Catalogue of the Greek and Etruscan Vases in the Department of Greek and Roman Antiquities, British Museum.* London, 1896.

——, *Catalogue of the Greek and Roman Lamps in the Department of Greek and Roman Antiquities, British Museum.* London, 1914.

——, *Catalogue of the Terracottas in the Department of Greek and Roman Antiquities, British Museum.* London, 1903.

——, *History of Ancient Pottery, Greek, Etruscan and Roman.* London, 1905.

Watzinger, Carl, *Griechische Vasen in Tübingen.* Tübingen, 1924.

Wernicke, *Griechischen Vasen mit Lieblingsnamen.* Berlin, 1890.

Wiegand, Theodor, and Schrader, Hans, *Priene—Ergebnisse der Ausgrabungen und Untersuchungen in den Jahren 1895-1898.* Berlin, 1904.

Winter, Franz, *Die Typen der figürlichen Terrakotten.* Berlin, 1903.

SPECIAL ARTICLES

Babelon, Ernest, Tête de nègre de la collection Janze au Cabinet des Medailles. *Gazette Archéologique,* IX, 1884, pp. 204-207.

Bates, W. N., Scenes from the Aethiopis on a Black-figured Amphora. *Transactions of the Department of Archaeology, University of Pennsylvania Free Museum of Science and Art,* Vol. I, 1904-5, pp. 45-50.

Bethe, Erich, Zu den Alabastra mit Negerdarstellungen. *Ath. Mitth.,* XV, 1890, pp. 243-245.

——, Der berliner Andromedakrater. *Jb. Arch.,* I, XI, 1896, pp. 292-300.

von Bissing, F. W., Mittheilungen aus meiner Sammlung—Kopf eines Libyers. *Ath. Mitth.,* XXXIV, 1909, pp. 29-32.

Bosanquet, R. C., Some Early Funeral Lecythoi. *J. H. S.,* XIX, 1899, pp. 169-184.

Brunn, H., Über die Ausgrabungen der Certosa von Bologna. *Abh. d. Mün. Akad.,* 1888, 18, p. 168.

Buschor, Ernst, Das Krokodil des Sotades. *Mün. Jb. Bild. Kunst,* XI, 1919, pp. 1-43.

BIBLIOGRAPHY

Calza, Guido, Expressions of Art in a Commercial City—Ostia. *J. R. S.*, V, 1915, pp. 164-172.

de Chanot, E., Bronzes antiques de la Collection du Duc de Luynes. *Gazette Archéologique*, V, 1879, p. 209.

Chase, George H., The Shield Devices of the Greeks. *Harvard Studies in Classical Philology*, XIII, 1902, pp. 61-127.

Deane, Sidney N., An Ancient Marble. *Bulletin of Smith College—Hillyer Art Gallery.* May, 1920, pp. 4-6.

Dressel, H., and Milchhoeffer, A., Die antiken Kunstwerke aus Sparta und Umgebung. *Ath. Mitth.*, II, 1877, pp. 293-474.

Engel, Arthur, Choix de tesseres grecques en plomb tirés des Collections atheniennes. *B. C. H.*, VIII, 1884, pp. 1-21.

Evans, Sir Arthur, The Palace of Knossos. *B. S. A.*, VII, 1900-1901, pp. 1-120.

——, Recent Discoveries of Tarentine Terra-cottas. *J. H. S.*, VII, 1886, pp. 1-50.

Furtwängler, Adolf, Antiken in den Museen von Amerika. *Bayer. Sitzungsb.*, 1905, pp. 241-280.

Gardner, Percy, Countries and Cities in Greek Art. *J. H. S.*, IX, 1888, pp. 47-81.

Graindor, Paul, Les Vases au nègre. *Musée Belge*, XII, 1908, pp. 25-30.

——, Tête de nègre du Musée de Berlin. *B. C. H.*, XXXIX, 1915, pp. 102-112.

Hartwig, P., Κεφαλὴ Αἰθίοπος μετὰ τῆς ἐπιγραφῆς Λέαγρος καλός. ᾿Εφ. ᾿Αρχ. 1894, pp. 121-128.

Helbig, Wolfgang, Vasi di Busiri. *Annali*, 1865, pp. 296-307.

Heydemann, Heinrich, Mittheilungen aus den Antikensammlungen in Ober- und Mittelitalien. *Halle Winckelmannspr.*, III, 1878.

——, Pariser Antiken. *Halle Winckelmannspr.*, XII, 1887.

——, Terracotten aus dem Museo Nazionale zu Neapel. *Halle Winckelmannspr.*, VII, 1882.

Mayer, Maximilian, Lamia. *Arch. Zeit.*, 1885, pp. 119-130.

——, Noch einmal Lamia. *Ath. Mitth.*, XVI, 1891, pp. 300-312.

Milliet, J. Paul, Les yeux hagards. Note sur une mode artistique de l'epoque alexandrienne. *Mélanges Nicole*, pp. 357-366.

Pagenstecher, R., Calena. *Jb.*, XXVII, 1912, pp. 146-173.

Panofka, Theodor, Delphi und Melaine. *Berlin Winckelmannspr.*, IX, 1849.

Perrot, Georges, Le Triomphe d'Hercule. *Monuments publiés par l'Association pour l'encouragement des études grecques en France.* Paris, 1876.

Petersen, E., Andromeda. *J. H. S.*, XXIV, 1904, pp. 99-112.

142   THE NEGRO IN GREEK AND ROMAN CIVILIZATION

Petrie, Flinders W. M., Naukratis—Part I, 1884-5—*Third Memoir of the Egypt Exploration Fund*, with chapters by Cecil Smith, Ernest Gardner and Barclay V. Head. London, 1886.
———, *Naukratis*—Part II, by Ernest Gardner. London, 1888.
Prinz, Hugo, Die Funde aus Naukratis. Beiträge zur Archäologie und Wirtschaftsgeschichte des VII. und VI. Jahrhunderts v. Chr. Leb. *Klio-Beiträge zur alten Geschichte, Beiheft*, VII, 1908.
von Prokesch-Osten, Anton, Inedita meiner Sammlung autonomer altgriechischer Münzen. *Denkschriften der Kaiserl. Akademie der Wissenschaften*, Wien, IX, 1859, pp. 302-334.
Puchstein, Otto, Die Sammlung Demetriou in Athen. *Ath. Mitth.*, VII, 1882, pp. 8-21.
Reisch, Emil, Vasen in Cornetto—Kopfgefässe des Charinos. *Röm. Mitth.*, V, 1890, pp. 313-322.
Reisner, George A., The Pyramids of Meroe and the Candaces of Ethiopia. *B. Mus. F. A.*, XXI, 1923, pp. 12-27.
Richter, Gisela M., Grotesques and the Mime. *A. J. A.*, XVII, 1913, pp. 149-156.
Robert C., Maskengruppen. *Arch. Zeit.*, XXXVI, 1878, pp. 13-24.
Seltman, Charles A., Two Heads of Negresses. *A. J. A.*, XXIV, 1920, pp. 14-26.
von Schneider, Robert, Neger. *Jh. Oest. Arch. Inst.*, IX, 1906, pp. 321-324.
———, Schlafender Neger. *Jb. Kunst. Samml.*, III, 1885, p. 3 ff.
Schrader, Hans, Über den Marmorkopf eines Negers in den königlichen Museen. *Berlin Winckelmannspr.*, LX, 1900.
Schreiber, Th., Alexandrinische Skulpturen in Athen. *Ath. Mitth.*, X, 1885, pp. 380-400.
von Stern, E., Ein Bronzegefäss in Büstenform. *Jh. Oest. Arch. Inst.*, VII, 1904, pp. 197-203.
Trendelenburg, A., Anfora rappresentante Perseo ed Andromeda. *Annali*, 1872, pp. 108-130.
Trivier, S., Tête de Chef Libyen—Bronze de Cyrene. *Gazette Archéologique*, IV, 1878, pp. 60-62.
Tümpel, Karl, Die Aithiopenländer des Andromedamythos. *Jb. Phil. Paed. Supplementband*, XVI, 1888, pp. 129-216.
Wace, Alan J. B., Grotesques and the Evil Eye. *B. S. A.*, X, 1903-4, pp. 103-114.
Walters, H. B., Odysseus and Kirke on a Boeotian Vase. *J. H. S.*, XIII, 1893, pp. 77-87.
Winnefeld, H., Alabastra mit Negerdarstellungen. *Ath. Mitth.*, XIV, 1889, pp. 41-50.
———, Das Kabirenheiligtum bei Theben III—Die Vasenfunde. *Ath. Mitth.*, XIII, 1888, pp. 412-428.

INDEX

Achilles, 7, 42, 45, 48.
Acrobat, 104, 105.
Aegina, 17.
Aeschylus, 4, 5, 6, 53.
African Chieftain, 73, 75, 76, 78.
Αἰθίοψ, IX, 2, 35, 117.
Ajax, 45.
Alexandria, 12, 77, 78, 79, 92.
Alexandrian hair arrangement, 79.
Amasios, 45.
Amasis, 43, 45, 46, 48.
Amazons, 51, 53, 55.
Amenophis, 8.
Ammon, 8.
Andromeda, 1, 6, 8, 42, 54, 55, 56, 62, 113, 118.
Antilochus, 6, 7, 42, 46.
Antioch, 78, 80.
Aphrodite, 2, 54.
Apollo, 75.
Apollonius Rhodius, 5, 6.
Apotropaic, 19, 20, 47.
Arctinus of Miletus, 7.
Asiatic Ethiopians, 5, 51.
Attic, 30, 34, 37, 42, 56, 67, 68, 70, 115.
Auctor ad Herennium, 117, 119.
Basalt, 101.
Bath slave, 103, 117.
Boxer, 85, 112.
Busiris, 13, 14, 15, 21, 28, 36, 42, 56, 57, 58, 103, 113.
Cabiric, 59, 60.
Caeretan, 13, 19, 21, 22, 56, 64.
Calliades, 34.
Camel, 64.
Camirus, 16, 17, 20, 81.
Campanian, 78.
Caricature, 15, 35, 59, 60, 61, 62, 77, 78, 80, 81, 93, 98, 113.
Carnuntum, 94.
Carthage, 120.
Cassiopeia, 6, 8, 54.
Cepheus, 6, 8, 54.
Charinus, 25, 27, 32, 33, 34, 36, 37, 39.
Charioteer, 103.

Charon, 64.
Chest of Cypselus, 35.
Cicero, 119.
Circe, 59, 60, 61.
Cnossus, 10.
Comic Interest, 37, 39, 44, 47, 56, 65, 81.
Cretans, 10, 11.
Crocodile, 37, 38, 39, 40, 67, 69, 70, 81, 94, 104, 112.
Cyprus, 13, 15, 19, 21.
Cyrene, 75, 78.
Dancers, 94, 96.
Delphi, 75.
Divers, 95, 126, 128.
Dolichocephalic, 58, 90, 132.
Double axe, 48-51, 57.
Ear-ring, 18, 19, 20, 58, 73.
Egypt, 1, 7, 12, 42, 51, 52.
Eos, 2, 6, 7, 42.
Epilycus, 32.
Ethiop Pelike, 64, 65.
Ethiopia, 7, 8, 9, 11, 20, 42, 54, 55, 118, 120, 133.
Ethiopian as an advertisement, 51, 52.
Ethiopian river, 4.
Ethiopian trumpeters, 46, 47.
Euripides, 5, 6, 8, 36, 55, 57, 113.
Execias, 43, 46, 65.
Fikellura, 14.
Filigree work, 106.
Florus, 119.
Fountain figure, 104, 105.
Funerary, 21, 80, 83.
Furious, 118.
Genre, 62, 72, 78, 80.
Grotesque, 35, 44, 57, 60, 62, 77, 78, 79, 84, 113, 124.
Hadrian, 133.
Heliodorus, 6, 8.
Hellenistic period, 77-114.
Hera, 59.
Heracles, 13, 14, 15, 21, 28, 36, 56, 57, 58, 103.
Hermes, 54.
Herodes Atticus, 133.
Herodotus, 5, 6, 10, 51.

143

144 THE NEGRO IN GREEK AND ROMAN CIVILIZATION

Hesiod, 3, 6.
Hesperides, 4.
Homer, 1, 2, 3, 4, 6, 7, 9.
Hunchback, 78.
India, 4, 117, 119.
Ink-wells, 125, 126.
Ionic, 13.
Iope, 8.
Iris, 2.
Italian imitation, 67.
Janiform, 11, 15, 22, 24, 25, 28, 29.
Joppa, 8.
Josephus, 8.
Juvenal, 118, 119, 120.
Lamia, 35, 42, 59.
Lampa, 121-124.
Laocoon, 38.
Leagrus, 23, 34.
Libya, 42, 58, 75.
Libyan, 3, 10, 35, 59, 76.
Ligurians, 3.
Literary tradition of Ethiopians, 6.
Lysippan, 75.
Maenad, 36, 39, 40.
Macrobius, 120.
Magna Graecia, 67.
Marathon, 51.
Martial, 118, 120.
Mask, 85.
Mauretania, 130.
Maurus, 118.
Medusa, 8, 54.
Memnon, IX, 1, 2, 4, 6, 7, 8, 36, 42, 43, 44, 46, 47, 48, 52, 53, 54, 103, 133.
Menelaus 2, 3, 45, 46.
Meroë, XII, 38, 39, 109.
Miletus, 12.
Mime, 113, 114.
Minoan, 10, 12.
Mimnermus 4, 6.
Moretum, 116, 119.
Naturalistic treatment, 35, 78, 79, 83, 113, 115.
Naucratis, 12, 13, 14, 19, 21, 30, 36.
Negresses, 25, 28, 29, 34, 35, 59, 60, 62, 70, 71, 72, 83, 84, 85, 96, 106, 107, 109, 111, 125.
Nereids, 54.
Nestor, 7.
Niger, 117, 118.
Nile, 4, 12, 36, 38.
Niobid, 86.
Nubia, 10.
Nubian, 87.
Numidia, 130.
Nymph, 36.
Odysseus, 2, 60.
Olynthus, 72.
Omphale, 36.
Ovid, 54, 118.
Pathos, 80, 90, 98, 112, 113.
Pausanias, 1, 7, 35, 59.
Pendant, 18, 20, 86, 106, 114, 129.
Pergamene School, 80.
Pergamum, 78.
Perseus, 8, 54, 55.
Persia, 7.
Persian Wars, 53, 115.
Personification, 55, 130.
Petronius, 79, 120.
Phineus, 54, 58.
Phrygian, 51, 58.
Pliny, The Elder, 6, 120.
Polygnotus, 36.
Poseidon, 2, 54.
Priene, 80, 83.
Procles, 25, 31.
Prognathous, 11.
Prometheus, 4.
Prophylactic, 20, 21, 81, 106.
Quintus of Smyrna, 4, 7.
Race prejudice, 37, 119, 120.
Realism, 77, 79, 80, 81, 111, 133.
Rhodes, 13, 19, 21, 78.
Roman attitude toward The Ethiopian, 119.
Russia, 80, 107.
Sardinian gems, 73-75.
Satyr, 26, 36, 40, 59, 63.
Scarabaeus, 17, 18, 19.
Scylla, 68.
Scythes, 32.
Scythians, 3, 51.
Seal, 18.
Senegalese, 11.
Silver inlay, 94, 97, 99.
Singer, 97-98.
Slavery, IX, 9, 21, 36, 37, 55, 62, 63, 64, 111, 115, 116.
Sophocles, 8, 56.

INDEX

Botades, 26, 37, 39, 67, 81.
Spain, 52.
Statue of Ethiopian, 36, 37, 65, 111, 119, 120.
Steatite, 18, 19, 20.
Strabo, 1, 3, 4, 6.
Success of portrayal, 64, 65.
Susa, 7.
Table attendants, 119, 120.
Tanagra, 79.
Terence, 114, 116.
Terminal figure, 129.
Thebes (Egypt), 8.
Thebes (Greece), 59.
Theophrastus, 10, 37.
Theseus, 63.
Thetis, 42.
Tibullus, 117, 118.

Tithonus, 2.
Town Mosaic, 10.
Tricephalic Agate, 109.
Trojan War, 45.
Troy, 7, 53.
Two-fold Ethiopians, 1, 5.
Use of Mould, 32, 33, 34.
Utilitarian attitude of Romans, 115.
Vase in form of Ethiopian's head, 15, 23-37, 70-72, 81, 88.
Vergil, 118.
Vocal Memnon, 7-8.
Weights, 126, 128.
Xerxes, 5, 10, 11, 12, 51.
Zephyrus, 2.
Zeus, 2, 59.

145

www.ingramcontent.com/pod-product-compliance
Lightning Source LLC
Chambersburg PA
CBHW051835090426
4273 6CB00011B/1809